A MYRIAD
OF DARKNESS

A MYRIAD
OF DARKNESS

Jamila Wiley

To order additional copies of this book, contact:
Xlibris Corporation
1-888-795-4274
www.Xlibris.com
Orders@Xlibris.com
85976

DEDICATION

I would like to give a special acknowledgement to Nora.
She inspired me to write this story.
Thank you, for supporting me and believing in me.
This would have not been possible without your encouragement.

CHAPTER 1

Nadia had arisen, in the middle of the night from a terrifying nightmare. She begins screaming and shouting, "ahhh!, in a horrifying tone of voice". Her eyelids lifted and the whites of her eyeballs nearly bulged out of their sockets in disbelief. Nadia sat straight up in bed and clutched onto her blankets. The pit of her stomach fluttered and her entire body tightened from a surge of adrenaline rush. She wiped the sweat from her brow, and hearkened faintly to an eerie sawing sound coming from her backyard. She hesitated to get out of bed, and pull back the drapes to take a look outside her window. It sounded like someone was wielding a chainsaw, slicing and cutting shrubbery in her densely overgrown backyard. The sound of the blade intensified. Whoosh! Her bed begins to suddenly oscillate violently for several seconds, and the shaking movement subsided. She shouted, "whoa Earthquake!" "Boom bang!" Instantly, a cogent jolting force had repositioned her bed, and made a vigorous clatter. Soon after, the light fixture on the ceiling begins to flicker on and off. "Crash!" Her picture frames on the wall hurled across her bedroom nearly striking her, and it shattered into several pieces onto the floor. A few seconds later, a caustics smell of sulfur began to permeate her bedroom. She became frantic and she began searching around to see if something caught on fire. When she discovered that there was no fire at her home. She returned back to her bedroom to call her friend Laura; to see if she felt the aftershock from the alleged earthquake. However, the shrilling sound of a chainsaw begins to continue to echo impetuously throughout her apartment. She began screaming and gasping for air. An ice cold chill begins to shiver down her spine. Perspiration was streaming down from her brow and her heart rate was beginning to profusely beat rapidly. She bolted from out of her bedroom and shouted, "who's there who is out there?" She swiftly walked to her window. She nervously probed outside. She saw an image of an obscured shadow behind the trees. She rubbed her eyes in disbelief and glared at it a second time. The shadowy figured hastily disappeared. Every muscle in her back and shoulders begins to tighten with dire fear. The stress in her face was visibly apparent. The lurking dark shadow deterred her so much that she dashed towards the front door as fast as she could wearing nothing but her pajamas, leaving her car keys and purse behind. She wanted to get out of the house as quickly as possible. Her roommate Shirell was standing at the front door; fidgeting with her keys before entering the door. She found the right key to the door and begins to open the front door. Nadia exits the front door, as soon as it opened. She was frightened too see someone standing there. When she realized that it was Shirell, she begins to incoherently explain what had happen that night. Shirell shouted, please slow down Nadia, I can't understand you. Nadia calmed down a bit and regain her composure. She asked, "Shirell, did you feel that earthquake tonight?" "What earthquake Nadia?" My bed veered across my wooden floors. My picture frames flung across my bedroom nearly swiping me, and shattering into pieces onto my floor. I smelt smoke in the air, and I heard the sound of a chainsaw slicing and rearing in the backyard. I also thought I saw a black shadowy figure lurking in our backyard. In my dreams, I saw myself walking down a street inlayed with black and white swirl patterns in the middle of the road. The sky was red and the boulevard street signs where written in reverse. I also saw visions of unprecedented patterns that you would never find here on earth. The dream felt tangible and real. I was walking down a street trying to find my way home but I couldn't find our street. Suddenly, a ghoul jumped out at me and I woke up. Nadia, yes that was a bizarre nightmare you had. I'm sure what you think you might have seen in the backyard, were some bushes swaying back and forth in the yard. The bad nightmare you had tonight is causing your mind to play tricks on you; It probably has something to do with the chainsaw noise you heard too. I don't think anyone would be using a chainsaw this time of night. I swear Shirell; I had just woken up when I heard it, and smelt the smoke. How do you explain my bed shifting across my bedroom floors, Shirell? Nadia, maybe there was an earthquake and I just didn't feel it. That is what it sounds like you've experienced. "I think you were partially asleep when you heard that chainsaw sound, Nadia. Get some rest I'm here if you need me. Nadia laid there in bed panicky for the entire night feeling uneasy; gaping out of the window and anxiously glaring into the harvest full moon. She was unable to clear her mind of the hideous dark shadow and the earsplitting roars of the chainsaw. Her subconscious mind was racing all night long. She didn't know what to expect next. Nadia became very antsy. She began to toss and turn in bed, and she was unable to fall back asleep. The fear and shock overtook her mind. She glared at her clock a second time, and it was now 4:00 a.m. A thumping force clouted against her home. Her big brown eyes quickly widened and dilated, and she began to shudder. A frigid chill came over her entire body. She quivered rapidly and walked back over to the window to peer into the darkness in her backyard. She sighed in relief that nothing was there to frighten her. She returned back to bed. She kept on her lights for the reminder of the night. Ms. Goldstein reached for the remote control and turned on the television to divert her thoughts from the terror. She had to question her own sanity because of the strange and sinister events that occurred that night. Nadia soon began to doze off and fell back asleep. The telephone began to ring resonantly and it had startled her. She was in a slumber and completely baffled. She answered it. "Hello, the caller paused, who is it, Nadia begins to ask?" This is Kadri. Ma'am, can I speak to Sarah please? "Kadri, Sarah doesn't live here." "I'm so sorry, ma'am," I must have the wrong telephone number." She muttered, "okay," and she hung up the telephone. She was exhausted. She lay in bed staring at the ceiling in a deep daze, reminiscing about the horrid events that transpired that night. She sluggardly climbed out of her bed and walked to her closet. She pulled out her sacred relic, a brass plated crucifix, and hung it on the wall just above her bed to appease the spirits. She lay back down in bed and closed her eyes. Minutes later the alarm clock sounded, and it startled her. She hit the off mode and lay back down. An hour later, she woke up from her sleep; she had overslept. She hopped out of bed and took a quick shower. She wore her white lab coat with a pair of relaxed blue jeans. She quickly slipped on a pair of white lace tennis shoes and headed out the door by 7:30 a.m. Her work schedule began at 8:00 a.m.

While on her lunch break, she was running an errand. She was standing in line waiting to be assisted, and a physically fit young man made his way over towards her. He uttered, "hello, my name is John." You look familiar. Do you live around here?" "No, I live about twenty miles north from here," she replied. John checked her out from head to toe. "I just want to let you know that you are an alluring lady." She smiled. "Thank you for the compliment." He asked, "Are you married?" She replied, "no, I'm not married, I've never been married before." He gazed at her in amazement and smiled with his eyes. "I'm shocked that a woman like you isn't already taken. Well, I date occasionally. I'm really busy most of the time with work and school; I don't have time for anyone. "How about you? Are you single, John?" He responded, "oh yes, I'm a single man." By the way, what is your name? I didn't think to ask you for it in the first place." He shook his head. "I apologize for that. However, it's a pleasure to make your acquaintance." She smiled and replied, "likewise it's a pleasure to meet you." She shook his hand and said, "My name is Nadia Goldstein. How is your day going, John?" "Excellent!" He nodded. "Where do you work, she asked?" "I work out of town for a large corporation. I'm an engineer. I'm currently on a vacation break spending time off with my kids. How many children do you have, John?" "Oh, a boy and a girl ages twelve and fifteen." "Do you have any children of your own, Nadia?" "No I don't, John I would like to soon one day though." Do you work here in town, Nadia?" She answered, "yes, I Do. I work for the local hospital down town. I work as a Laboratory Assistant. I have been on my job for a while. I'm also a part-time student. I'm working on getting my degree as a Biologist." "You look like the scientific type, are you trying to help find a cure for loneliness, he jokily asked?" "Are you trying to be a comedian, she responded and chuckled." "I enjoy working in this field." I choose to work in this field because I wanted to help find cures for all sorts of conditions mainly cancer. He asked, "Is it possible that we can exchange telephone numbers?" I would like to get to know you better." "Of course we can," she replied." She was eager to meet him. He immediately contacted her. The caller id speaker phone announced his name, and she quickly answered the telephone. As soon as he begins to speak, the sound of his voice aroused her curiosity. She wanted to devour him badly. A deep sigh sound slipped from out of her glossy plump lips. She begins to fantasize about when she first met him. His dark complexion reminded her of a bowl of hot fudge, drizzled on top of some vanilla ice cream, on a warm sunny day. "Wow, he could possibly be the one for me. She mumbled underneath her breath." They had been talking well over an hour in the early morning. He offered to take her out to a lunch, movie, and a party all in the same night. She wanted to get out of the house and take a break from studying and working all week. She agreed to go out with him. He pulled up to her home and rang the doorbell. She opened the door on the third ring. She stepped out of her apartment. His jaw nearly unhinged and fell to the floor as soon as he saw her. He had to take a second glance at her. She wore a long flowing streamline faux fur shawl, with a black silk spaghetti strap dress. Her dainty bangles and royal blue sequined clutch bag were in coordination with all of her accessories. Nadia was ecstatic to step out into the town and be noticed. He adored her classy outfit; he was pleased with her persona. He was glad to accompany her. He complimented her several times about her exceptional beauty. He had stroked her ego, so she had immediately begun to vivaciously dance around in front of him. "I see you're going to be the life of the party tonight, go ahead and dance then with your bad self, he replied." Her initial thought was to remove away, all awkwardness and tension; that may come with the first date. They proceeded to walk on the sidewalk to his Mercedes Benzes. She wore a pair of black four inch tall pumps, that had a tinged of royal blue. The drenching rain had dwindled away a half an hour before he arrived. She nearly slipped and fell upon the wet leaves and uneven pavement. He quickly reacted, and grabbed her before she slid down and hit the concrete like a softball player skidding into home base. They merely laughed so hard, that they could hardly catch their breath. "I would have ruined my dress and scraped the meat off my knees, if it wasn't for you saving me, thank you, John." It was their first date together; she wanted him to feel comfortable and relaxed around her. "Please don't you mention what just happen to me to your friends okay, John?" He opened up his eyes wide like the size of a saucer. He held his stomach and chuckled. "I want tell a soul babe okay." He was laughing inside because he knew she was feeling extremely good about herself, but he didn't mean any harm by doing so. They continued to walk to his car. He muttered," You're almost the same height as me in those heels." She stood about five-feet-nine inches tall without heels. She smiled, "well at least you're taller than me by two inches, John". She had a medium built frame, with magnetic dark brown eyes. Her personality was caring and charismatic. Her smile was contagious and her looks where exotic. Her bone structure in her face was long and sharp. She could have been a high fashion model in her youthful days, but fate has changed its cards. She was exuding with elegance, pose, and confidence. He took her by the hand and helped her get into the car. "Where would you like to go eat, Nadia?" I know of several places I can take you but, I'd rather let you designate." Well, actually I'm open to wherever you want to go, John." You're a really easy lady to please. I admire that about you." How about I take you to a steak house? He then murmured, excuse my French, but I'm famished." I feel like I could eat them out of house and home." He laughed. "How about you, Nadia?" She nodded her head yes, and said," I'm a bit hungry too." John smiled, "well, let's get out of here and get something to eat." They drove up to the restaurant. They walked inside, sat down, and viewed the menu. The scenery was beautiful. There was a waterfall in the middle of the eatery, after lunch, they went to the movies and watched an action-packed saga. He asked her, "Do you mind, if we stopped by my place first; so I can freshen up for the party?" Maybe you can watch television while I'm getting ready?" I'm not trying to pressure you into doing anything. I would like to also sit down and maybe we can have a solo conversation at my place. I live alone, nobody lives with me. My son and daughter come to visit me every other weekend. He asked, "do you have a problem with me being a single dad?" Nadia placed her soft manicured hands on his face and gently said, "absolutely not!" "I can only imagine how demanding it must be. Being that you're a single and responsible dad, living on your own." I can appreciate your dedication to your children and I admire you even more for doing that. This world would be a better place, if there were more active role models like you. He smiled, and cracked a joke, "you can have them their all yours to keep." He lifted his arms in the air smiling happily. "Thank you for your support." I will tell you the truth; It was a difficult decision to make. Separating two kids from their parents." Also, too have our kids in different homes is a struggle." Even though, I tell them every day, how much I love them, and they could talk to me about anything that might be on their mind. They seemed to be adjusting okay to our separation. They were in tears at first when I left our home. It was hard for them initially but there strong kids. They have seen over the years how me and my ex-wife were at each other throats, fussing and fighting verbally. My kids are very understanding. I'm a proud papa. However, me and my ex-wife are on better speaking terms now, and we have seemed to be at a more solaced peace than ever before, for the kids sake. They needed to observe mommy and daddy being cordial to one another. We grew out of love with each other we argued like cats and dogs every other day. I didn't want to raise my kids in that chaotic environment anymore. I just could not bear it any longer my kids where suffering from it. That is what caused our separation in the first place. Since our divorce we get along even better. We support one another; she has moved on and found a partner in a new correlation. John mentioned, "I didn't mean to carry on like this being that this is our first date." I must mention, eventually this would of came up sooner or later." So, I figured I should address it immediately. I just want you to know that, I'm no longer married. I'm not hiding any secrets from you. I'm a single dad. I'm not really looking for anything serious right now." However, I do want to mingle and see what the world has to offer me, he stated." I recently purchased my home about seven months ago in the city of Antioch. It's my little quiet and peaceful retreat. She asked, "so John what do you like to do, on your spare time?" I'm an athletic person, Nadia, I jog, play golf, and ride my motorcycle". She later asked, "so do you belong to a motorcycle club?" He responded yes I do, me and my buddies like to ride our bikes on the weekend. "Pretty lady, what do you like to do on your spare time?" "Well I'm a physical fitness junkie; I enjoy cooking. I love the beach scene; I always go to the beach in the summertime, just to lie on my beach towel. With an oversized straw hat. Tarrying on the ocean front soaking up the sun rays. I enjoy sipping on a tall glass of cold lemonade on a hot blistering day. They later return to his place. He took her on a tour around his home. His place was warm and cozy. His color scheme was beige chocolate brown with a touch of blue. He has a small dinette nook in his dining room. It was a single level home with four bedrooms. He had a hot tub in his backyard. He proudly displayed his college degrees that he had received on the fireplace mantle. She congratulated him for his achievements.

"How much time do you have left in the clinical science program, he asked?" "One year, I'm actually in the clinical aspect of my training." It's a lot of hands on experience. It's interesting to see the many different types of amoebas under the microscope." He asked her to make herself comfortable. He went to the kitchen, poured her a glass of wine, and they sat down and began to talk. He was a good-looking man. He was thirty-seven-years-old, single, and respectful. Unfortunately, he divorced his wife a couple of years earlier. He didn't want to rush into marriage again. He was looking to have a good time, and so was Nadia. "John, do you think you would ever get married again, Nadia asked?" "Yes Nadia, but I don't want to rush into marriage." I want to wait until a few years from now. I want to make sure that I find the right person to settle down with. I need to discover who I am first; maybe I also need time to heal from my prior situation. Nadia, would you like to watch a movie now?" She said, "sure I don't mind!"

He had a collection of movies he had stored away in his entertainment center. "I will put on a movie it's a romantic comedy. I haven't had a chance to watch it because of my hectic work schedule. I hope that you will enjoy it. Please sit back, kick up your feet, and make yourself feel at home."

He sat next to her and he dimmed the lights. He put the video into the dvd player. He went to the kitchen and popped some sweet and salty flavored popcorn. He headed back into the living room and asked, "would you care for some water?" He grabbed a couple of bottles of icy cold spring water from the refrigerator. I will take a quick shower, and will come back to see about you. Here is the popcorn, and enjoy the movie okay. The movie started off comical she had a few laughs. Twenty minutes had gone by, he came from out of his bedroom smelling like fresh soap and cologne and it was getting late. "He stated, "It's about time for us to go to the party". "Are you ready?" Let me walk you to your car, but first let me grab your coat. It's sort of nippy outside. "Do you want to drive together or take separate cars? "I rather ride with you if you don't mind John". "Where is this party located, she asked?" "It's in San Francisco a forty five minute drive from my home, he answered. My friends rented out a lobby hall in a Hotel Inn and their throwing him an annual bash. It's his thirty-fifth birthday party. They enter into his vehicle and begin to drive in town. He asked, do you need anything before we get to our designation. She mentioned, "well, if it's possible, can we stop by the convenient store down the street from your house so that I could pick up a bottle of red wine to bring as a gift for your friend. They pulled over to the store she got out and pick up a bottle of sweet red wine, breath mints, and water and they began to ride down the highway interstate. He turned up the radio and put on some smooth jazz music. There was a complete utter silence while driving to the party. They enjoyed the music and wanted to observe the high rise buildings and the city lights. The traffic was heavy; it was bumper to bumper on a Saturday night. While driving he took his eyes off the road for a second, too looked into her eyes, and said," You have the most beautiful biggest brightest eyes, I have ever seen." She blushed and looked straight out through the windshield and screamed, "John stop the car! "watch out!" He nearly rear ended the person in front of him. The car in front of him was skidding and breaking out of control. "John pumped on his breaks and changed lanes quickly, to avoid hitting the car in front of him. "Nadia that was a close call; that is why I always leave a car length space between each vehicles. They continued on their route and they finally made it safely to the hotel. He drove up to the valet parking and he got out of the car. He approached the passenger side where she sat and he opened Nadia's door. He reached for her hand and she stepped out of the car, and they entered the lobby. There were a lot of new faces standing outside the door. There was even more of a crowd inside of the hall. He held her hand while they walked inside the hall looking for his childhood friend, Joe. He spotted his friend Joe sitting at a table eating a meal. Joe stood straight up, "what's up John? How are you doing man, how have you been?" I'm cool everything is fine, Joe!" I've been working a lot not really able to get out much and socialize. Anyhow, Joe, I want you to meet a dear friend of mine, Nadia", Joe approached her and gave her a hug and smiled. "I'm Joe, glad to meet you. "Nadia where are you from, he asked?" She answered, "I'm from Fresno, happy birthday Joe!" I brought you a bottle of sweet wine to celebrate your birthday, Joe." "Awe Nadia, you didn't have to do that for me." Joe smiled and thanked her. She handed him the bottle of red wine. He asked, "are you guys hungry?" Help yourself over there to the buffet bar there is plenty of food. I suppose we can go for some food and dessert. John stated. John asked Nadia, "would you care for some dessert and food?" Sure, I'll find us a spot to sit Nadia, while you go fetch us a plate. Nadia grabbed two plates there was so much food to choose from, she didn't know where to begin. She turned around and glanced across the entire room looking for John. He waved his hands in the air and she spotted him. She walked over to the table and joined him. They dine on garlic crab with cake and ice cream. The band begins playing music and they got up from the table and begin dancing. They party that night. John's close friends from his neighborhood and classmates from his college university were there. They mingled all night and a beautiful woman approached John and begins to flirt with him. Nadia came back from the bathroom after reapplying her makeup on her face. She walked up to John, and said hey John, who is this? The woman rolled her eyes at Nadia. She frowned, and looked at Nadia from hair to her shoes. She said, "John, I will catch up with you later okay." She walked away with a glowering look on her face. Nadia reacted rational and did not say anything back to the rude woman. She told John, "she didn't have to disrespect me like that." It's your friend's party and I'm not going to cause a scene. If I see her again on the streets; I will tell her a thing or two about herself. John said, "Nadia don't worry about her, she's nobody special". They left the party after midnight. They made it back safely to his house and walked her to her car. "You know you can sleep over, I got that cozy couch you can sleep on," He replied. John, I rather be in my own bed tonight, I will have to come back to visit you another time. In the back of her mind, she thought about her policy not to sleep with a man or spend a night over his house until he passes her test. Did you have a good time, John asked? Of course I did, you made me feel comfortable and welcomed. Nadia, thanks for coming with me, I never like to travel alone. I hope we can do this again soon, he said." Thank you, John; I had a wonderful time with you even though Ms. Jealousy tried to ruin the party for me. "What! "Don't worry about wasting your time thinking about her, please don't, Nadia." I know John, I want John, thank you for inviting me to spend the night over, but I can't right now. By the way, how much money did you spend on the bottle of wine? Oh, it was some cheap sweet wine. "I hope he will enjoy it John." Don't be silly, Nadia. "I'm sure he already opened the bottle and is enjoying it right now." He's not rude person, he is a friendly guy, and he would appreciate it. Well, let me walk you over to your car since you don't want to stay at my place. "John, why did you say it like that, in that tone of voice? No honey, I'm just joking; once you get to know me you will know that I'm not really that serious okay. I'm not trying to entice you to come over. I'm offering you the choice to do so. Let me open your door so you can get inside the car and turn on your heater. You have a long drive ahead of you. I want you to be safe knowing that you had a few drinks tonight. So hurry up now and get into your car okay. He opened the car door for her. She smiled and gave him a hug, and he gave her a peck on the neck.

On their fifth date, they held hands and walked on the beach coast. He took her by surprise. He grabbed her by her waist and landed her in the sand on her bottom. "John, what are you doing to me? You're embarrassing me, pick me up and help me get back on my feet this instant please." He grabbed her and wrestled her near the murky blue ocean. He wanted her to loosen up a bit, so he rolled her around in the sand and gave her a peck on her lips. He picked up a bundle of intertwined green and brown orange coral reef and showed it to her. She didn't want it near her. She ran away from him in disgust, and he threw it back into the deep sea. They were placid on their beach chairs. They watched the wave crash against the rocky coast and the sun set below the horizon. He licked his lips and asked, "are you hungry, Nadia?"

She responded, "Sure, what do you have in mind, John?" He said, "how about some Thai food?" She muttered, smiling, Thai sounds great."

They packed up their belongings and headed for the restaurant. They dined that evening at a gourmet restaurant, and the food was great. They return to his car. He cleared his throat and said, Nadia, I want to let you know you're special to me, and I want to develop a closer bond with you." She said in a soft tone of voice, "I feel the same way about you. Perhaps, we should spend more time together." I like the idea. However, there is something I want to share with you. I hope that you don't get freaked out by what I'm going to tell you. I was born and raised in the island of Jamaica. My grandfather was a medicine man from there. When I was a young boy, my grandfather would take me to the deep forest to collect different herbs for rituals. He was a sought-out man in our village. He was a natural healer. He helped heal people with many diseases. My grandfather taught me many amazing things. It is my belief, when a human being dies, their soul can enter into animals' bodies.

She uttered, "what did you just say? Damn, John, I never heard about that before. He merely laughed. Yes, it's true. But don't worry. Nadia, it's only a wise tale. She wondered if this myth was coming from his grandfather." She was astonished about what he had told her. Later that evening at John's place, Nadia went upstairs to grab an extra blanket from the second bedroom. The bedroom windows were open, and the sheer curtains were whirling around in the wind. She walked over to close the window and looked outside and she saw a dense red fog hovering over John's backyard. She rushed down the stairs to tell him what she saw. She yelled, "John, hurry up, go over to the window, look outside and tell me what do you see." Nadia said in a blaring tone, "I just saw a red cloud floating low just above your car garage and traveling towards your backyard window. She was terrified about what she had seen. He didn't believe her. He questioned her, "are you sure you saw a red fog floating in the air, and it wasn't a reflection of something, Nadia? He shrugged his shoulders in disbelief and walked over to the window to see what was going on. He replied, there's nothing out there, honey!" John, I just saw a red cloud hovering over your backyard. I saw it for several seconds. I know what I saw. It was there. Please believe what I'm telling you. I wouldn't lie about something like that. She uttered, maybe it was a reflection after all."

She prepared a home cooked southern meal the following day. She cooked fried chicken, collard greens, mashed potatoes, and gravy, with a homemade apple pie. She finished washing her hands, and looked up and glanced outside the kitchen window. She saw the neighbor waving his hand at her. He was standing inside of his kitchen gazing at her. She focused in on him and noticed something else was strange. The entire kitchen area was pitched black, and it was only twelve o'clock in the afternoon. It looked sinister. It looked as if it where twelve midnight. She could not rationalize or comprehend why the blackness lurked throughout the kitchen. The shutters were completely pulled back, and the sunlight was let in. She didn't have a reasonable explanation why this was occurring. These people clearly wanted to scare her. She kept her eyes on the neighbors. She started to wash the dishes, and she saw a woman walking like a zombie. Her head was slumped down, facing the ground. She laggardly walked across the backyard in a slumber. Nadia could see the woman through the spaces between the fence. Suddenly, a man appeared from out of nowhere. His appearance was ghostly. His skin was pale, and his height was seven feet tall or more. He held a shovel in his hand. His torso reached the top pointed edge of the fence. He stood parallel with the fence. He knew she was watching him, although he never moved his head to look in her direction. He stood motionless for a long period of time. It sent chills down her spine. John made it home from shopping and was there just in time to see him. Nadia shouted, "John, come and see your weird looking neighbors. "John dropped his keys on the countertop and looked at the young man and said, "he's weird to stay in that position for that amount of time without any movement. Nadia, please walk away from the window. And please help me carry the grocery bags in the house." Nadia gasped. "Sure, honey. What did you buy anyways?" "I brought wine and dessert for tonight."

Later that evening, after dinner they took a short walk around the neighborhood. John uttered, "thank you, Nadia, for cooking that meal for me. It was truly delightful. We need to walk because this will fatten us up." "Well, I'm not worried about my girlish figure. However, walking sounds like a plan," They began to walk down the road. She asked, "so, how was my apple pie?"

Before John had a chance to answer, Nadia uttered, "oh my lord, look up, John." She saw a huge black bird with a wing span of ten to fifteen feet in length. It was sitting on a fence near an open field where cows graze. They came within ten feet from it. It took off and flew up into the sky. It was stalking the cattle. This reminded her of those stories people would tell when their cattle are found mutilated. "I can't believe what we just saw, John. I know, babe. What we just witnessed was rare and unusual." She uttered, let's turn around and go home." They made it home safely and went back to the kitchen to put away the food that had been cooling down. They helped each other in the kitchen as a couple. He went to his refrigerator to get the wine. He pulled out two chilled wine glasses from out of the freezer and poured the wine into the glasses. They began to drink and talk about what they had seen.

Several months later their relationship took a turn for the worse. He cheated on her, and she had caught him in the act. She drove up to his house to surprise him. He came to his front door with sweat pouring down from his brow. He told her that he had a guest over and that she wasn't welcome to come into his house. The look on his face was obviously deception. She walked towards him, and he pushed her back outside the door. She had a key to his place, but she didn't use it in the first place. If she did, she would've walked in on him and her together doing who knows what. She asked him, "who is this person?" He replied, "A friend of the family." She stated, "I want to meet your guest." He frowned, no you can't Nadia." "Why can't I?" He uttered, we're busy." "You're busy doing what, John? He then closed the door in her face. She hit the door and left him. She didn't have it in her heart to leave him for good, but she did let him know that she wasn't going to take that kind of treatment anymore. She definitely meant what she was saying. She knew he was definitely lying about his guest. She decided to give him a second chance to straighten out his act. They stayed together after the incident. Nadia and John decided to work on their relationship. They took a short vacation together. They traveled to Lake Michigan. They drove down to Lake Michigan and stayed for three days. They secluded themselves that weekend. They turned off their cell phone and enjoyed each other's company. The resort had a swimming pool and a hot tub. "Honey, there is a nip in the air." They immediately entered the hot tub. "John let's scurry and get inside of the hot tub and look up at the stars in the sky." She wore a two-piece black bikini that showed her chiseled abs. She had been working out on a regular basis; she jogged and lifted weights. Before entering the jacuzzi, she felt the temperature of the water with the tip of her toes. The moonlight shimmered beneath the surface of the water. As they entered the water, she asked, "how many stars do you think are up in the sky, John?" He chuckled and said, there are countless, Nadia." He took a sip of his apple martini and began to tread the water. He embraced her and gazed into her big brown eyes and kissed her. They had been in the hot tub well over an hour. The steam from the water exhilarated them. He helped her out of the spa, and the water poured off her toned frame. He asked her, "do you want to go to the restaurant and get something to eat?"

She concurred, and they went back to the room to change their attire. She wore a pair of comfortable blue jeans with a black halter top. They walked over to the pizzeria and ordered a large combination pizza. They brought their pizza back to their condo, and she opened the champagne bottle. "This was a romantic evening don't you think so, Nadia? "Yes, it is John." In the morning, let's stop by the lake and then go to the dock to watch the boats sail, Nadia." The next morning they woke up bright and early to the sound of birds chirping and the sun shining through the window pane. They drove to the lake. "Look at the lake John, doesn't it look calm and refreshing?" She kneeled down to touch the blue sudsy water. John, waved his hand at a passing couple nearby. He responded, "sir or madam, do you mind taking our photo please?" "It's certainly not a problem sir." "Are you from around here?" No, we're just visiting." John, handed the couple the camera. "thank you very much for your time, and taking our photo, John said. The wind started to pick up; Nadia, long flowing white dress blew around in the wind. She pulled her loose hanging curls back into a ponytail. The breeze and cold air made her curls droop. John was warm. He wore a thermal underneath his long-sleeve shirt. The weather was chilly; it was wintertime. They could observe the snow on the mountaintop.

They had been driving for miles. He stopped at a hillside to make snowballs and play with the children. John had a great sense of humor. "John let's go shopping. I want to pick out a few items for friends and family. "They drove down by the pier to the shopping center, and it was crowded with people. They stopped at a couple of outlets. She purchased some souvenirs and T-shirts. After browsing, they had been exhausted and went back to their room. The suite was plush. Inside of the bathroom was black granite towel, and supersized jetted Roman tub. The kitchen had a subzero freezer, and a wet bar. On their last night they hated to leave. They wanted to take another trip down that way again. They stayed for breakfast in the morning before they left town.

When they returned home from their trip, she discovered that he wasn't going to change or be committed to her. A woman came to his home, pounding her fist on his front door. Nadia uttered, "who is that, John? Are you going to answer it?"

He hesitated to answer the door. She heard a woman saying in a raucous tone, "Open up this door, John." He opened up the front door. He nervously asked, "Why are you banging on my front door? Will you please calm down a little bit?" She said, "Where have you been? I've been calling you for several days and you won't answer me." He replied, I've been gone out of town." She muttered, "You been out of town, and you didn't bother to inform me." Nadia was infuriated, she ran to the front door. Both women stared at each other and at the same time said, "Who is this woman, John!" I'm Marla. I've been dating John for the past year. And who are you?" Nadia, and John is my man. Why are you here?" She walked up to him, slapped him on side of his face, and stormed off. She blurted out, "He is a lying, cheating, no-good man. You can have him, Nadia." John told her, "You better hurry up and leave my property, and don't you come back because I will be calling the cops. "Nadia was aggrieved. She asked him, "Why did you embarrass me like that, John? You have been seeing this woman behind my back. Don't you thing that was a shallow thing to do to me? I think it's time for me to go too." She slammed the door and said, "screw you!" He opened the door. "You got the nerve to talk to me in that tone of voice, Nadia. Have a good life, John. I'm done with you. It's obvious that you're not going to take me serious or our relationship serious. I'm out of here." She shouted, I will find someone else who will be true to me. I do not have to put up with your cheating anymore." She fled off and drove away. On the way home, she was in a deep muse. She had little hope for relationships. She was fed up with his crap. Nadia had little hope for being in a new relationship. Nadia thought it was impossible to find a good man. She was fine with being alone. At least she didn't have to put up with the drama anymore. She was amazed how he didn't try to fight for her love. He just let her go, and she could tell by his reaction that he wasn't her true love. The relationship was nothing to him. All the years she had spent with him trying to make it work was all in vain for John.

CHAPTER 2

Nadia told Maleya everything. She was frustrated with Nadia. She told her that she realized she had been going through it with John. She told Nadia, "It's going to hurt you for a while, but you really must try to get over him. I told you before that he was no good for you. Please listen to me. Everything will be okay. Let's get out of the house and go to the nightclub tonight."

"Maleya, I'm not really feeling up to it, although I could use a drink."

"Yes, I could use one too myself. You read my mind, Nadia."

When Maleya and Nadia entered the nightclub, all eyes were on them. The club was jam-packed with single people. They received compliments as they passed by the crowd. Nadia wore a V-neck plunge blouse with a short Minnie shirt. Her stiletto heels looked perfect with her outfit. Maleya wore a colorful printed leggings with a clingy half top shirt that showed her six pack abs. They were looking to have a good time that night. Nadia let hair down; it was long and curly. Nadia and Maleya headed straight for the bar. The bartender asked them what they will be drinking. Nadia muttered, "I just broke off my relationship with my man. I need you to fix me a stiff one please." He replied, "I got you covered. I'll take care of you." He frowned and said, "don't worry yourself about him. A good looking woman like you will have no problem finding the right one. I hope you enjoy this drink. Cheers." Nadia ordered two shots of Brandy. After she finished her drink, she started to dance on the dance floor solo. She was moving and grooving. She noticed a man sitting at a table in the corner beholding her. He walked over to her and asked her to dance. She smiled and said, "okay, well, let's dance." They started dancing and he asked, "what is your name?" She shouted, "I'm Nadia." He pulled her close to his body and whispered in her ear, "I'm Boris."

"It's nice to meet you, Boris! They're playing my favorite song. Let's party, Boris. You're a great dancer."

Nadia was feeling good, and she began to cut loose. They were both having a ball on the dance floor. He grabbed her by the hand and said, "Come and sit with me." They walked over to the table and sat down. She grabbed a napkin off the table and wiped her forehead from the sweat flowing down her face from dancing all night long. She could see Boris face clearly under the lamp shade. When she saw him, she was very pleased. There was an instant attraction. He was tall; he stood about six feet three inches in height. He was handsome. He had dreamy grayish slate eyes. He was a socialite, and she admired that about him. "Nadia," Boris said smiling, "could I buy you a drink? What will you be drinking?"

"I'll take another shot of Brandy, Boris." He walked over to the bar and brought her back her drink. "I'm sorry, Nadia." He pointed at someone. "I have to go see about my buddy over there. He had a bit too much to drink. He's inebriated. I will look for you later, Nadia."

"Go, Boris, I understand. Please go and take care of him." She grabbed her glass and took a sip. She glanced over the entire floor and spotted her friend. She seemed to be having a fun time. She was on the dance floor swaying her hips. Maleya got discovered for writing romantic poetry. Maleya is no introvert Nadia has been to a couple of her performances. She had been booked to perform at many places. Maleya's dream is to write poetry for a living. Maleya is a very talented woman. Nadia wished that she could be more like her having a carefree upbeat spirit.

At that time, Nadia wasn't searching for romance, but it had found her. She figured that she wasn't getting any younger, so she would give him a try. She thought many of times that she would grow old and be lonely. Her past experiences were getting the better of her. Every relationship in her past that she'd been in turned out to be wrong. She has been cheated on all her life. She felt like nobody could satisfy her. After the club closed, she saw Boris outside. He was sitting in his car. He pulled up next to her and said, "hi, sexy lady, can I give you my telephone number?"

"Okay, if you don't bite."

"I don't bite, Nadia. You're safe with me."

"Here is my number. By the way, Boris, how is your friend? Is he okay? Where is he?"

"He left home with his wife."

Nadia shook her head and said, "I'm glad he is okay and everything."

"Yes, he's fine. He just needs to go home, get some rest, and sober up. It's been nice meeting you, Nadia. Call me so that we can get together. I'll treat you out to dinner." "Okay, I will put your number into my cell phone for safekeeping. "I will call you, Boris." "Have a good night and drive safely."

She walked to her car and thought to herself that she wasn't going to rush into things with him. She was going take it slowly.

A few months went by. She was looking through her cell phone contact list, and she saw Boris's number and decided to give him a call. She called him and said, "Hello is this Boris?"

"Yes, it is."

"How are you doing?"

"Hey, long time no hear. I've been waiting for you to call me. Wait; please don't tell me your name. This is Nadia, right?

"Yes, you remember me?"

"I'll always remember your sweet, sexy voice."

He was excited to hear from her. She was impressed that he remembered her name. "Could I take you out to dinner tonight? I'd like to show you a good time."

"Sure, why not? It sounds like a plan."

"What time are you coming to get me, or should I meet you there?"

"It's up to you, baby, whatever you're comfortable with."

She thought about it quickly. "I'll meet you there. Boris, where are we going?"

"I want to take you to that Italian restaurant downtown." She looked at her watch, and said, "I know exactly where you're talking about. What time should I meet you there?"

"Let's meet at 4:00 p.m. Is that cool with you, Nadia?" "That will be fine with me, Boris. I will see you there."

"All right, pretty lady, I will see you soon."

"Okay, Boris, by the way, I will be driving a black range rover."

"Okay, I'll be looking for you. I can't wait to see you, Nadia."

Hours later, she met him at the restaurant, and he flashed his headlights as soon as she drove up into the parking lot. He walked over to her car and opened the car door for her. She could smell the aroma from his cologne as he reached out to give her a hug. The first three buttons on his shirt were open. She could see his chest; it was broad and muscular. He had a huge smile that spread across his face. His voice was deep and manly. He muttered, "I'm glad you could make it."

She said, "Thank you, Boris, for coming out to meet me here."

He replied, "You're welcome. It's my pleasure!"

She uttered, "I'm glad to be out of my house."

"Well, I'm glad that you made it here, Nadia. Are you ready to go inside and eat?"

"Yes, I am, Boris."

He held onto her waist and they walked inside the restaurant.

They entered the restaurant. He pulled out a chair for her. She sat down, and they began to chat. The waiter came to their table, and he asked, "what will you both be drinking?" She said, "a glass of cola will be fine with me." He drank a cold beer. She grabbed the menu and began to read it. She ordered lasagna with a salad. He ordered a plate of spaghetti with meatballs. As they began to dine, she asked him, how was your day? Oh, uneventful Nadia. And yours?," Well mines was very busy." How is your spaghetti? "He replied, "It's actually great."

The sauce dripped onto his shirt. She reached for a napkin and dabbed it. "Oh, man, look at me. You have to excuse my manners. I can't believe what I just did."

She smiled and said, "Relax. It's only a stain. You can wash it out."

"So tell me, Nadia, how was your lasagna and salad?"

"I enjoyed my lasagna. It was very moist and tasty and the salad was fresh. Did you enjoy your dinner too, Boris?"

"Yes, it was better than I expected, even though I dripped spaghetti sauce on my shirt. I will be back here soon."

"Thank you, Boris, for treating me to dinner. I owe you one. It will be my treat the next time we go out together." After dinner, they walked back to their car, and he asked, "Nadia, I know you just met me, but I was wondering if you would like to come over to my place for cocktails?" She answered, "Boris, I don't know if I can make it."

He touched her shoulder and said, "I'll make you the best drink in town. You have got to come over and try it."

She shrugged her shoulders and said, "well, okay. I won't be able to stay that long, Boris."

"Not a problem, Nadia. I was planning to go somewhere myself tonight. Please follow me to my place. I won't drive too fast for you."

She followed him home and walked into his place. It looked like a bachelor's pad. He had leather couches with pictures of his family on his coffee table. He told her, "Make yourself at home. Get comfortable. I will go to the kitchen and fix you a drink." He handed her a martini and he warmed up a plate of balsamic wings. He muttered, "so, tell me a little bit about yourself."

She answered, "well, I'm a student, and I work for a hospital. I'm a Laboratory Assistant."

She asked, "so what do you do for a living, Boris?"

He replied, "I'm an antique collector. I work for myself. I own my own business." He folded his arms and asked, "so you're a student?"

She replied, "Yes, I'm fascinated with microbiology. He said, "That's a rewarding field. Best wishes to you. May I ask this, do you have a boyfriend?"

"No, I'm single. However, I ended my relationship a few months ago."

He asked, "What happened?"

"It's a long story. I'm not sure if you want to hear about it."

"Actually yes, I do want to hear about it. I have plenty of time to listen to you."

She replied, "Well, he wasn't ready to settle down with me. He had an affair, and I ended the relationship and that was it."

He smiled and said, "My ex-girlfriend and I recently broke up."

She asked, "What happened?"

He replied, "We grew apart. We couldn't agree on anything. But we are on better terms. We have to be for our child's sake."

Boris asked, "Have you ever been married before?"

"No, I haven't. Maybe someday I will be. But for right know I'm okay with being single." She tasted the martini he prepared and muttered, "Umm, that was refreshing. This taste so tangy Boris. What did you put in it?"

"I added vodka and some other secret ingredients."

"Come on, Boris, you got to give up the recipe."

"Well, when you come back next time, I will tell you."

"Okay, Boris, I will take you up on that offer. I really want to know how you were able to put it all together and make it taste so good."

He said, "Thanks, Nadia, I'm glad you enjoyed the drink. I told you that you wouldn't be disappointed."

She looked at her watch and shouted, "Oh no. Look at the time. We have been talking for a couple of hours. I must be going home." She could feel the liquor sneaking up on her. "I really think it's time for me to go, Boris. Thanks for everything."

"You are welcome. I'm really glad that you were able to stop by. Did you enjoy the drinks?"

"Oh yes, they were very delicious, Boris. I would ask you for a third glass, but I have a thirty-minute drive."

"Yes, you do have a drive ahead of you. Nadia, I want you to be safe too. Let's meet again, Nadia. I will cook you a special dinner next time."

"You're a chef too, Boris?" she asked and said with a smile, "I'm looking forward to that.

He muttered, hey Nadia come over here next to me. She smirked, and walked over to him. He grabbed her and gently held her in his arms. He softly nibbled on her red luscious lips. She could feel her heart palpitate. He squeezed her firm perky breast ever so gently. He told her that he needed her, and that he would never leave her. He laid her on his sofa and ran his fingers through her hair. He continued to kiss and caress her. The sweat feverishly poured down his brow and dripped onto her perfumed scented ivory skin. While making love to her, her body quivered in ecstasy. He spent the evening satisfying her every fantasy. "Boris, it's getting late, I must go now". She uttered, "okay, let me walk you to your car. Let me grab your jacket first, Nadia."

They walked to the parking garage. He held her hand and said, "I will call you tomorrow."

He embraced her and gave her a peck on the cheek. She left for home that evening and was feeling good. She thought that she had found a compatible man. However, he wasn't perfect and had a few flaws, but that was okay. She had flaws herself. She didn't want to rush things with him because he had gotten out of a long-term relationship with his child mother. She hesitated about dating him. She didn't want to be involved with a man who just got out of a long-term relationship.

On her way home, she called Maleya and asked her for her advice. She told her," I just met a man who recently got out of a relationship with his daughter mother. Should I pursue him or not?" Maleya told her not to waste her time. Nadia stated, I just made love with him tonight. I usually don't rush into things like that. You know me girl, I'm usually shy and you know about my policy, not to sleep with a man until he passes my test. That policy flew out the window tonight, Maleya. However, the mood was right, and it just happened. I enjoyed it. There was an insane strong chemistry between him and I, Nadia said. "Girl, I don't have a good feeling about him, my gut is telling me something different Nadia. At that moment, she didn't know why she would judge him so quickly or pick up on the negative vibes on him without meeting him. Although her friend told her it wasn't a good idea, Nadia went ahead and dated him. She thought that she should give him a chance. Maybe he will turn out to be the best one for her. Nadia dated him. He was good to her; she could trust him. They dated for twelve months, and she found no problems of infidelity with him.

He would shower her affectionately with flowers and gifts. He would also call her on a daily basis. One day, she fell ill. He called her and said, "I haven't heard from you all day. How are you doing today?" Before she could open up her mouth to talk, she let out a big sneeze. "I'm sick."

He softly said, "You are? Could I bring you some soup, honey?"

No, thank you, Boris. I don't want you to catch my cold."

"Are you sure? I'm in the neighborhood."

"I'm sure. I want to lie down and get some rest."

"I agree with you. Get some rest. Take care of yourself, and I will see you soon."

She felt good knowing that he wanted to take care of her. She was glad that she had met him. She thought that he was great and that no other man could take his place.

A few months later, Nadia came across a woman named Tori Madison. She graduated from high school with her. Tori was the busybody type. She stopped Nadia in the grocery store. She muttered, "I haven't seen you in a few years. How have you been?"

Nadia answered, "I'm fine."

Nadia asked, "How are you and your family doing?"

Tori replied, "Just fine. But why are you glowing, girl? Are you married?"

Nadia answered, "No, I'm not married."

"Well, who's the lucky guy? It's written all over your face."

"I'm in a relationship."

Tori asked, "What is his name?"

"His name is Boris."

She asked, "Boris who?"

She looked at her and thought this lady needs to mind her own business. "His name is, Boris Grayson."

"She said, in a loud tone of voice, Boris Grayson!" I know him. I'm sorry to tell you this, girl, but you better watch out for him."

Nadia, looked at her perplexed. "What are you talking about, Tori?"

She said, "In time you will figure it out."

At that point, she was angry. She had no idea what to think or who to believe. Boris gave her no reason to question him, but she had a feeling that she should look into it. Nadia went to Boris's home, and he was on the telephone being secretive. He was isolating himself in the room on the telephone with the door closed. She put her ear on the door and she heard him say, "Man, I'm a single man. I can do whatever I choose to do. I want to meet her."

She ran away from the door with tears streaming down each cheek. She didn't confront him that night on this because she didn't want to believe it was true. She didn't want him to know that she was eavesdropping on him. However, she gave him the cold shoulder all night long. He kept asking her what her problem was. When he tried to kiss her, she pulled away from him. Nadia knew she had to catch him in the act in order to call it quits. A few weeks had gone by since the incident. She was shopping at a clothing department store, and she saw Tori again. She was heading in her direction with another woman. She overheard Tori saying to the other woman, that Boris wasn't the right guy for her. Boris was seeing other women and that he was not in love with her. He was just using her. Nadia's mouth hit the floor. She instantly knew that Boris was guilty of doing this. She was disappointed that it got back to her in that way. It didn't surprise her that she heard Boris had been cheating on her. She had a hunch that he was two-timing her. She was angry that word got back to her from Tori. She was outraged that Boris had been talking badly behind her back. It confirmed her suspicions that he would do something like this to her. She didn't hesitate to call him. She asked him, "What have you been telling people about me?

He said, "What are you talking about?"

She sighed and said, "I was in the store and your name was mentioned. Tori and some other woman mentioned something about you and I." Boris uttered, "What did they tell you?"

"It doesn't matter what they've told me. It's what you've been saying about me." She shouted, "Why did Tori say that you're using me? Do you even care about me?"

He answered, "You know I care about you!"

She said, "I don't believe you. I heard you on the phone a couple of weeks ago saying you're single and you can do what you want to do. And who is this woman you want to meet?"

He replied, "You don't know what the hell you're talking about. You've been listening to my conversation, and you didn't even hear the full details. You heard the tail end of my conversation."

"Boris! I don't want to hear any more of your excuses. I don't think this relationship is going to work out anymore. I want out of this relationship because I can't trust you. You have made me an unhappy woman, and you have given me a reason to believe that you're being deceitful. I can't trust you anymore."

He replied, "If you don't trust me, then you can walk away if you want to. But it's your fault since you want to believe everything people tell you."

"Boris, you know you're lying. I heard you with my own ears. When I heard you on the telephone, I knew that you were a cheater. I made a mistake when I let you into my life. I don't want anything to do with you ever again. I don't deserve to be treated like this. Yes, I will walk away from you, but remember this, what goes around comes around!"

A couple of weeks after the breakup, Nadia was in her living room lying down on her couch with her windows wide open. She heard Boris outside talking to her next door neighbor. She waited for him to come to her door, but he never showed up. She assumed that he would come up to her place and apologize to her. He never came to her front door. She was upset that he had been around her complex, and she didn't have a chance to confront him. Later that evening, she heard a seductive whistling sound coming from her backyard. It was so entrancing that it made her skin crawl. It debauched her soul. She looked outside the window but, nobody was there. She wondered who it could've been. A few seconds later, she heard a voice saying, "come to me. Are you jealous?"

She was speechless. She didn't know where this voice was coming from. The voice traveled from beneath the floors. It seemed to be coming from her neighbor's place. She asked her roommate if she heard anything unusual that night. If it wasn't for her roommate Shirell living with Nadia, nobody could've paid her to stay there.

The following evening she returned home from work and lay down in her bed to rest. She closed her eyes and stretched out her legs. She hadn't gone to sleep yet. She was just starting to relax. Suddenly, her television turns on and off by itself three times. She reached for her remote control and checked the batteries and nothing was wrong. She figured the television had malfunctioned. She lay back down and closed her eyes and she heard a man heavily breathing next to her. It had inhaled and exhaled then let out a sighed. She could recognize its voice. It was, Boris's voice. However, she was the only person in the room, and she could hear him breathing heavily next to her in her ear. She leaped up and ran out of the room, shivering. She didn't know how to explain or why she could hear him breathing in her ear because he wasn't there in the flesh physically. She was in shock and denial. As she reached for her car keys and coat to leave the house in a panic she turned around too look back, she heard her roommate's door open up slowly creaking and then immediately slammed shut. She screamed and flew out the front door. As soon as she got to her car, she called Boris telephone number to see if he was at home. She wanted to confront him. She decided not to talk to him but to listen to his voice. She dialed his telephone number, he didn't die and had returned to haunt her. He answered his phone, he said, "hello,!" she hung up the telephone in his face. She was afraid to talk to him. She couldn't set foot in her room for a while. She lay on her couch for many nights because this had an effect on her. She would not stay home alone unless Shirell was there with her. She called her close friend Rick who is a minister. She explained to him in a frantic tone of voice that doors where opening and shutting by themselves. Also, the television turned on and off by itself. "Pastor Rick, I also heard the sound of my ex-boyfriend Boris voice next to me while lying in bed. However, he wasn't there physically with me. He said, "Listen to what I'm about to tell you, and believe me it's true. That sounds like demonic activity. It also has something to do with astral projection."

She uttered, "astral what? I never heard of it."

He answered, "It basically means your soul can leave your body to travel anywhere in the universe. It is also known as an out-of-body experience. Witches who use astral projection method use it to travel the world."

She uttered, "So you're telling me he's a witch, and he can travel in spirit and come inside my room to haunt me."

"Yes!"

She uttered, "are you serious, Pastor Rick?"

"Believe me. It's true."

Nadia fell silent. She said, "Is this why I heard him sighing in my ear last evening?"

"Yes, it is very well possible, and be very cautious of him. This is an ancient sacred Egyptian belief."

She told Pastor Rick, "I got out of a relationship with him a few weeks ago. I don't have anything to do with him anymore. However, he has been coming to me in a vision and dreams. I had no idea why I was seeing him in these visions. He would come to me and make himself known. I was able to see him in a vision because he is a witch."

"Yes, Nadia."

"Pastor Rick, I never practiced witchcraft or dabbled with the occult."

"Be glad you didn't, Nadia. It's possible that he has something to do with it. He may even be a fallen angel from hell who is here to wreak havoc on earth."

Nadia replied, "a fallen angel? Is he here to destroy me?"

No, Nadia, he can't destroy you because the Lord is on your side."

"Could a mere mortal man be a dark angel in disguise?"

"It's conceivable. This is why you have seen the supernatural visions. He uses his powers to try and scare you out of your mind. Be very cautious and stay away from him. Do not give him the opportunity to get near you. I won't pastor, Rick.

"What am I supposed to do? I was in a relationship with him, and he never did anything unusual. He didn't levitate or expose his powers to me."

"Of course he won't, Sister Goldstein. He didn't want you to know about it. Now that you're out of the relationship with him is being subtle about it. He is a crafty, maleficent fiend from hell." Is my soul damned? "Did I commit a damnable sin, Pastor Rick?" "No Nadia, you're not damned."

"What does he want from me?"

"That's something you may never figure out, but remember that he is not of this world. He has cast his lots with the devil. You need protection. Go and get baptized and pray. Stay away from him. He is dangerous."

"Pastor Rick, I have nothing to do with him anymore. I will take heed and go to church for prayer. Do you think he has put a hex or a spell on me?"

"It sounds like it. He has put something on you. No ordinary person should be seeing the things you have witnessed."

"He has put a curse on me, Pastor Rick. I was in my room one evening praying. My legs felt as though they were on fire. I reached for my legs and rolled all over the place. The burning sensation was so intense I began to cry out for help. I didn't understand why this was happening to me. I saw a flash of lightning, and I heard a vibration sound near my bedroom window. I thought my guardian angel was communicating with me. I asked him to stop the burning sensation, and it stopped. I then asked him what was heaven like. I could hear waves crashing and birds chirping. It was so serene, I believe that he showed me a glimpse of paradise. Pastor Rick, I'm not for sure who was communicating with me at that time. I don't know if it was my guardian angel or not showing me these things.

"Be very wise about it. Do not fall into his trap. He is not of this world, he is of his father, the devil. He is trying to manipulate you into thinking he's your guardian angel. He is not one of the Lord's angels."

"Pastor Rick, I'm glad my roommate heard me crying. If it wasn't for her, I don't know what would've happened to me. I felt very weak in there. I saw nothing but darkness fading to black. When my roommate entered my room, I think I was losing consciousness. I felt as though I was going to pass out. I thought that I was going to disappear and be swept away into the unknown."

"He definitely was trying to take your soul. I'm glad that you are still with us, Nadia."

"I'm glad to be here, Pastor Rick. I will never be a fool like that again. I will run for my life if I encounter a situation like that again."

"Nadia, these are the forces of darkness, and you can't fool around with them. I will be very frank with you. You almost lost your soul in there."

"Pastor Rick, something was overtaking me that day. I wasn't myself because I know I would've normally fled out of that room. It is hard to explain why I stayed in there and let it happen to me. It was like something was controlling me.

"Pastor Rick, another bizarre incident took place when I was at home alone and had an uncontrollable feeling came over me. I went to the kitchen to eat a bowl of spaghetti. I felt this animalistic urge to devour my food. I ate my food like a wild animal. My stomach began to billow as if I were pregnant. My seven-year-old niece told me that my stomach was big, but there was no baby in there. I was surprised that she noticed it too. I went to the doctors because of the swelling, and they told me it was gas. I returned home, and I saw five perfect dots in the palm of my hand. I don't know how the dots got there. I didn't put it there myself, and it looked unusual. The next day I was on an errand. As I was waiting in line, one of the associates from the store walked by me. She was mimicking me using her hands. She was acting as if she were putting food in her mouth, eating it wildly. This bewildered me because I did it in the privacy of my own home. How could she have known this? Do you think she's involved with them?"

"Nadia, what you just told me sounds very strange. However, you will be very surprised who is involved with Satan. You might be right—she may be involved with them. They say that the devil brings down fire from the sky to deceive many. You are a typical victim of witchcraft. Witchcraft is sorcery. It is used to cause harm and to torture men. It emerged in the 1000-1500 AD. Both men and women accused of witchcraft were burned at the stake. Woman was the main targeted victims of execution."

She asked Rick, "Do you think he has this much power?"

"I believe anything is plausible." She knew right there that she wasn't going crazy or it was a figment of her imagination. She always knew that he was out to get her. There were far too many unusual things happening to her. "Nadia, get your bible and begin to read Psalms 91 and pray. "I will be praying for you, sister."

Her life had made a 360-degree turn since November, and it had never been the same.

"I'm a rational woman, Pastor Rick."

"I know you are, Nadia."

"Something was telling me that it's Boris. The vision I saw of him was real. I'd seen many things, but my memory is sort of foggy."

"Nadia, don't second guess yourself. Of course it was him. What are you going to do about it? Are you going to listen?"

Nadia shook her head, and said, "Yes. That explains the voices. When I saw him in a vision, he was with a woman in a pool of water. He had his back turned away from me so that I couldn't see his face. But I could still recognize his profile. He started to do a dance and taunt me. I then saw a place surrounded with fire. I also saw many men who looked colonial with white wavy wigs on, sitting at a table in purgatory. I saw hundreds of men waiting at a table. I also saw two little girls in dresses with long hair. They looked like identical twins. My eyes where wide opened when I saw these visions. I don't know what all this means, Pastor Rick.

"Nadia, don't try and figure it out. Let the Lord fight your battles for you. Come back to church and ask for a special prayer."

"Okay, Pastor Rick. I will do that. In the meantime, take care."

"You take care too; Nadia It's always nice to hear from you. God bless you, Nadia. Call me if you need me. I'll be there for you, sister Goldstein."

"Bye, Pastor Rick."

These visions disturbed Nadia. She was looking through the sheer curtain and had seen a silhouette of a man in her backyard. She was frightened about what she had seen. During that time, she heard another voice; it was the sound of a heavenly deity outside communicating with the demon. The good angel was helping her to communicate her defense. The angelic angel said that she was a good person who was chastened and misunderstood. The angel called the demon by his first name, which was Boris. She then asked him, "Why are you doing this to her?" The fiend spoke telepathically to Nadia. His voice trembled and said the women he was with were better lovers than Nadia and that he would rather be with other women. Nadia answered, "why are you doing this to me, Boris?" He laughed and began to tap at her window with energy rays. She threw a blanket over her head and hoped that he would miss. She knew from prior experience he was aiming to strike her in her chest. He wanted to torture her with pain. She heard three different voices talking in her backyard saying, "join us, join us, join us." She knew right away they wanted her to give in to them and make a pact with the devil. She wasn't going to let it happen. She told them to leave her home and go away. She ran out of the room and told her family. She knew it was pure evil that she was dealing with. The haunting continued on a daily basis.

Chapter 3

Nadia was shopping at a local bookstore, and she was standing in line, waiting to make a purchase. Suddenly, from behind her, a large, tall young man dressed in all black started swinging his hands back and forth behind her back. He seemed to be invoking a spirit on her. He looked as if he belonged to some sort of witch covenant. She swiveled around to see what he was doing behind her back, and he immediately stopped. She caught him in the act, and he quickly walked away. She imagined he was sane, but then again you never can tell. She didn't know him or never saw him anymore. She was not sure why he did this to her. She could only imagine that he was up to no good. He must have known who she was because he was most definitely after her.

The following day, she went to a Laundromat to wash a couple of loads. She was folding her clothes when a woman walked inside the Laundromat with her basket in her hands and said, "those demons are going to get her." She was blown away by her remark. How could she have known what she was going through? Nadia was angry with her because she was indirectly talking about her. She was surprised to hear it come from out of her mouth, especially from an older and wiser religious woman. Nadia also felt a bit relieved, knowing that a credible person knew about it other than herself. She wished that this woman would someday advise her on what to do. She figured that the neighbor didn't want to get involved. It was still a mystery to her that they didn't know each other that well, but somehow she knew that the demons were out for her. Nadia muttered, "people know a lot more about you than you think."

She went home to relax after washing and folding her clothes. She sat on her couch, leaned over, and grabbed her cup of coffee that was on her coffee table and took a sip. She let out a big yawn and stretched out her arms. She looked out of her window and saw a huge invisible force split open the tree branches like a pathway to enter through. She was daunted. An invisible force was moving around in the tree. The branches bounced a few seconds and closed back up. She shut her curtains and tried to calm down. She knew it had nothing to do with the wind blowing the tree limbs around. Something had jumped into the tree to watch her. Later that night, she heard a woman moaning outside her door. She peeked out the peep hole and watched a crazed woman walk to her front door and try to open it. She didn't call the police, but she was grateful that she locked it. She didn't know what to expect. The next morning she saw fifty vultures nesting in her tree. She said to herself, is this a bad omen? Nadia heard a slithering snake near her front door. She wondered if someone put it there. Her neighbor would stomp around her entire her home. Nadia knew that this was an old Louisiana myth that was used to cast out evil spirits. Nadia started to stomp around her home. She was anxious to fix her situation, but it didn't work for her. She became so uncomfortable living there that she decided to move away. Her new place was peaceful for several months. Toward the end of the year, all hell broke loose.

She was out running an errand. Before she entered the freeway, she saw a homeless man who waved at her and covered his eyes with his hands. She was not sure what he was trying to tell her, but she saw a dead black cat on the side of the freeway and a couple more further down the road. She wondered if this was a sign for her. It was the end of November, and she was starting to see several unusual things again. She thought that she had been cursed because strange things were beginning to happen to her again.

One evening she was driving in her car, and she approached a stop sign. A 3X symbol appeared on it. She became inquisitive. She drove around the corner three times and stopped at the stop sign again. After circling the block three times, it disappeared right in front of her eyes. She headed toward the downtown city area. She was at a red stop light. A young man began to cross the street in front of her, waving his hand at the passenger seat side of her car. He said, "Hi, man, how are you doing, man?" This startled her because no one was sitting in her car. She thought maybe this guy was insane. The light changed, and she left the intersection and went home. She began to slowly drive her car through the neighborhood to observe the Christmas lights and decoration. As she passed by, the whole block of Christmas lights simultaneously turned off in sync. It seemed like a sinister force was controlling the electricity.

She committed herself into a psychiatric hospital because she could no longer protect herself from this entity. She initially told the doctor that she had been hearing and seeing things around her home. He evaluated her. She told him that she changed her mind about staying in the hospital. He then told her that she was under a 5150 watch and that she was unable to leave the hospital. She complied with the rules and stayed in the facility. She felt like she was no longer safe at home. She wanted to escape the torment. She thought that she would be safer in a hospital. However, the presence continued to follow her there. She could frequently hear the sound of chainsaw in the hospital at night. It startled her. It would get louder when she seemed to be frightened. She was so terrified to look down the hallway. She thought she would look into the eyes of whatever was after her and it would saw her into pieces. She was helpless against this entity. She knew she wasn't crazy. She never experienced hallucinations as a child. She hadn't had any psychological problems in the past. There was nothing that she could connect the dots to. If there were, she could get help for it. She could take medication to alleviate the problem. She knew her ex-boyfriend had hexed her. She had seen him in a vision, and that was enough evidence to convince her that she needed to escape him.

To her discovery, the entity followed her again to another facility. She was lying down in bed resting when she looked up towards the ceiling vent and saw "pure evil"—a demonic-looking owl. It had large piercing black devilish eyes. His menacing bane eyes were peeping down on her. She started sobbing because it was horrific. She couldn't contain herself. She couldn't move; she became paralyzed with fear. It was pure evilness. Nadia couldn't look upon its face anymore. She stared the devil himself in his awful eyes that night. He transformed himself into an owl. All she could think about while lying there were those horrid black eyes. It also made a tapping sound with its claws against the ceiling vent. It wanted her to look at him a second time. She wouldn't take a second look because this creature was dreadful. It shrewd intelligence, It tapped its claws against the ceiling vent to get her to look at it again. She just laid there in bed and couldn't move. She screamed aloud. She heard the staff say, "She must have seen it." How could they have known what she was screaming about? They knew what was happening to her. The nightmare didn't end there. Later, that evening, she was in the bed resting. Her room had an attached bathroom. She heard the sound of a growling dog inside of the bathroom. The snarling and growling was more intense than an ordinary dog—perhaps, a demon dog. No animals were allowed on the premises. So that ruled out any speculations of a pet. This was eerie. All she could do was hold her breath and pray that it wouldn't harm her. She was somehow able to go back to sleep. She abruptly woke up with a charley horse in her leg and couldn't move. The pain was tremendous. She turned to the right, and in the corner appeared a ghostly silhouette of a man. He approached her swiftly and touched her shoulder. She couldn't move. She closed her eyes. He spoke to her. His voice echoed, as if he were under water. He called her a "frog." She couldn't move or get up. She felt something pinning her down. From out of nowhere she saw him holding a baby in his arms. The lights turned on, and he disappeared. She then heard the staff say, "Happy birthday! Aw, you got ringlets in your hair. Are you hungry?" It was so creepy. It seemed like this child was hungry for human flesh. She had a strong feeling that they were going to enter into her room. She muttered, underneath her breath, "no, don't come in." She could hear them hesitate and walk away. The next day she reported that someone was in her room and they touched her. She had written an incident report. The nurse asked Nadia to come to her office. Nadia sat down and handed her the incident report. She read it and said, "tell me what happened."

Nadia said, "a man walked over to my bed and touched me."

She said, "who did it? Could you identify him?"

Nadia said, "no, he doesn't work here. But it did happen. It's the truth." Nadia knew that this had happened to her, but it was difficult for her to prove.

The nurse said, "If you can't identify him, then there's nothing more I can do." It was like talking to a brick wall.

The following night, Nadia was resting in her hospital bed. She heard heavy footsteps walking down the hallway and stopping at her door. Her door was slightly ajar, and she looked out in the hallway but didn't see anyone there. The heavy footsteps continued walking down the hall and exiting out the back door to the patio area. It sauntered outside and stopped near her bedroom window. She clutched her blanket, and her heart began to palpitate. In a blaring tone, he said, "Your time is up," and he fired three gunshots up into the sky. Nadia pulled back the covers from over her head and sat straight up. He quickly came back inside and stood by her door. She wanted to vault out of her room, but she was apprehensive about leaving. It entered into another room down the hall. It slung a bed and dragged a chair around with unimaginable strength. It left the room, walked back down the hallway again, and surceased at her bedroom door. She whispered, "oh my God, please help me. Please do not come in." It stood at her door scratching at its chapped or burned skin. She knew it wasn't mortal. It was a bad spirit trying to find a way to enter through the portal to harm her. He then swung open her bathroom door, and she saw nothing but pure darkness. She knew that evil was lurking, and she was horrified. She wanted to see her tormentor. She believed that if she was caught looking into his dreadful eyes again, he would take her body and soul straight to hell. The beast continued to stalk her until midnight. Some of her memory of what had happened that night had been blocked out to help protect her sanity.

She resided on the unit for a period of two weeks. She was initially there for a forty-eight-hour watch. When she stopped taking her medication, they extended her stay. Four to five staff members would be in her room to watch her receive her daily injections. She didn't take the medications that they prescribed her. She was paranoid about the medication because she had to take about ten pills a day. Each day she would wake up drained. Mentally, she was stable, but she was able to function. She had no relief. She felt like she was doing a jail sentence. When she prayed to her higher power, they laughed at her. The Lord was there to protect her. She isolated herself from others. She felt hopeless and perplexed. She lost twenty pounds from not eating. There were dark circles under her eyes from not sleeping. Her skin looked dull and blotchy. She wouldn't bathe for days and felt depressed. The patients complained about her hygiene. They made her wash up. When she left the hospital, she was bruised and sore from all the injections she received.

During her therapy session, she looked at all the artwork that was hung on the walls. She saw an image of the holy cross turned upside down, which represented Satan. She didn't know why they let it freely or visibly hang on the walls. But she thought that she better get out of there. They were glorifying Satan and his legions, and this terrified her.

The following day she was walking down the hallway in the hospital when a patient walked by her. She noticed that the side of her face had suddenly changed. It looked strange. It looked as if she had been burned in a fire. This patient purposely tried to scare her out of her mind and trick her into believing that her imagination was running wild. This was bizarre because she sat down at the same dining table for lunch the previous day, and nothing was wrong with her face. She had powers to disfigure her face in the presence of Nadia.

A few days went by, and she could hear another patient talking loudly, saying something was wrong with his back. She glanced at his back. He was sort of hunched back. He was wearing a hospital gown. The upper portion near his shoulder blades of his back was exposed; you could see his rashy red skin. As soon as she did that, she became faint. She thought that she was going to fall to her knees. It was unexplainable. It was like something left her body. He persuaded her to look at him so that he could harm her. She was astonished about what had happened. She had to drag herself over to the lobby water fountain and drink the water. Amazingly, she recovered from it. After all these events had taken place, she said, "I must find a way to get the hell out of this place and leave." She immediately told the charge nurse that she was having chest pain because she wanted to go to the local hospital. They had no choice but to send her to the hospital. She traveled by ambulance. They hooked her up to an EKG machine. As she was being hooked up to the EKG machine, the demeanor of the technician was quite crude. Nadia was the one suffering, and she could've been a lot more kinder.

Upon entering the hospital, she heard a technician say, "Look at her eyes. They look very dark." Nadia had no clue to who she was referring to. She then asked a technician for a glass of water. The woman said, "She was trying to seduce him." Nadia was offended. She ignored her comment, and she remained quiet. She kept her ears and eyes open and listened. Suddenly, a heavy fatigue came over her. She started to feel faint. She couldn't put her finger on what was happening to her. She felt like she was going to pass out. This was no ordinary sleep. She knew they were trying to do something to her. She couldn't keep herself from passing out. She was struggling to keep her eyes open. An older man in his seventies who was a patient there blurted out loud, "They're not going to get her." He must've known what was going on or knew that she had caught on to them. She drank about four to five glasses of ice-cold water just to keep afloat. She began to panic, and she started to pull off the EKG leads that were still attached to her body. Nothing could stop the faint feeling. She was running out of time. She was getting weaker by the minute. She looked down at her side and noticed she missed a few more leads that were still on her skin. She removed the leads, and when she did that, she could instantly feel her body snap back to feeling normal again.

A man who was sitting next to her was getting a gash wound sutured. He was trying to get her attention. He gestured several times to her using his hands and covering his eyes. She perceived and caught on to him. He was trying to communicate to her not to look directly into their eyes. She wondered what the hell was going on at the hospital. She had no other choice but to do what he showed her to keep herself safe. She would turn her head when they looked at her or head in her direction. Subsequently, her EKG report came back normal. They sent her back to the psychiatric ward. Meanwhile, she got back. She plotted her escape. She saw staff open the front door at the ward, and she took off as fast as she could to get out of there. But little did she know there were two other doors she had to get through to get out. Staff rushed after her. She scurried to the bathroom and locked herself in it. She heard them say, "Open up the door!" She refused to do so. They used their key to open the door. She climbed on the counter and tried to break the window. It was too high up for her to climb out of and escape. The casement was about a ten feet climb. She stood on the countertop to try and get out. She cracked the window but couldn't escape. She was fortunate that she was unable to escape because she could have been attacked on the streets.

CHAPTER 4

The hospital discharged her in January. The haunting continued two weeks after being released. She developed a twitching movement in her head. She would twitch backwards and forward. She had no control over the jolting movement. She left home and went out to get herself something to eat. She pulled up at a drive-thru restaurant and placed an order. While waiting for her food in line, she began to uncontrollably twitch her head backward. The vehicle in front of her hastily put their car into reverse. Their wheels started spinning and smoking. The more she twitched her head backward, the closer the car would get to her. It seemed as though he was going to back into her car. It seemed to be replicating her every movement—every time she twitched her head backwards, the car would drive in reverse. The adversary was controlling Nadia and the car in front of her. When she would twitch backwards, the car would drive reverse. So every time she jolted backwards, he would nearly back into her car. As she proceeded down the road, her head begins to jolt in reverse. And the car in front of her threw itself into reverse and skidded out of control. It nearly hit her car. She drove home and knew that it had confirmed her suspicion that the fiend was in control of the two incidents. She returned home that afternoon. When she was lying on her couch, she saw an eerie white-and-yellow light radiate throughout her apartment. She looked across the room, and on the wall appeared a form of a three-dimensional black triangle. It was approximately two feet in height, and it looked mystical. It scared the hell out of her. At that time, she didn't realize that these triangles were used as portals for demons to enter through. They are also used in séances to summon up high-level demons. The bible she had in her hand and she was reading, had a drawing of a black pentagram inside of it. It appeared on the top part of the page. She also saw an image of a cartoon figure. It had a face of a young boy on it. The bible wording had changed. Some of the vocabularies were from a Latin and an unknown inscription. It read that that she was going to be a bearing woman who was to be married to a sheep keeper. She felt as though this entity was going to take her back into another century. Perhaps, she would be lost somewhere in time forever. This was petrifying to her. She sat the bible down on the couch and tried to get up. She was unable to lift or move her legs. She was pinned down for roughly five minutes or more. She heard her front door knob twist as if someone was going to come into her home. She was running out of ideas. She then removed the blankets that were on her legs, and the heaviness left. She was able to get up on her feet. She figured that maybe if she lifted the blanket off her body first, she would be able to get up and walk. She was stuck on the couch, and by doing so, she was able to get up. It was her belief that Boris came over to her house and made contact with the same blanket that was on her legs. His energy was on this blanket, and somehow he was able to manipulate his powers by touching the blanket. He concocted this whole scheme. She left her apartment quickly and rented a room for the night. She took a hot long bath, and she wrapped the towel around her body. She walked over to the mirror and stood there seconds to look at her face. Her tongue had a mind of it's own and begins to slithered uncontrollably like a snake. She ran away from the mirror and sat on the bed. Approximately 12:00 a.m., she was awakened by the sound of pounding and banging noise on the walls at the hotel where she stayed in. The sound would grow louder and get closer to her. She jumped out of the bed in her pajamas and got into her car. The pounding continued in her car. So she parked, and looked and searched inside of her vehicle. But she didn't see anything. When she returned to the front seat, her car key was gone from the ignitions.

The entity took her key from out of the ignition. She looked on the ground and inside of her car for them, but they were nowhere in sight. As she walked away, a man drove into the parking lot. He was blasting loud music. He was playing the song, "Go dummy, go dummy." He then asked her to come over to his car. She was alone. Nobody else was in this parking lot. She didn't respond to him. She kept walking in another direction. She had a strange feeling that he knew something about her car keys. He probably wanted to offer her some sort of a deal. She didn't want any part of it. She didn't care about material things. She knew that her car key could be replaced, but not her life. She walked the streets for about an hour trying to find another room to rest in. She carried her umbrella with her to use as a weapon. And it started to pour down instantly on her. There was no rain in the forecast that day. As she continued to walk, she threw the umbrella down in the alley. She was outraged and shocked that it was in control of the weather. As she was walking to the phone booth, she looked down on the ground and saw the pavement lit up as if there were electricity in the ground. The pavement would display shapes and patterns; the ground would glow with every step that she would take. Another man pulled over and asked her if she needed a ride. She told him "no thank you," and she proceeded down the street. She suddenly saw in the distance a huge diesel truck driving in her direction, and it disappeared instantly before it passed her. She kept on walking, and she could hear the sound of frogs croaking very loudly in the pond. She wasn't tired. She was mystified about what she had seen on her way to the hotel. She didn't want to return home because of what happened to her earlier. She was afraid to go home. She didn't want to bother anybody and asked them if she could stay at their place. She rented a room. She went inside of this room, and five minutes later, the pounding started in this new room. Before entering the room, she saw a man dressed in all-black apparel watching her enter the room. He entered the room alongside of her room, and she could hear him through the walls. The pounding on the walls continued. She knew she had to do something fast or figure out what she had done wrong. She threw off all the blankets on the bed onto the floor. She shouted, "I wish someone would help me." She heard the man inside the other room yelling at the top of his lungs, saying, "yes, yes, woo!" She knew that he had heard her, and he was up to something. This alarmed her. She wanted to leave the room. She left the room and lost money on both rooms that night. It comforted her knowing that she still had her life. She had seen the man come out of his room and watch her on the balcony in the distance. She went to the main office to use their phone, but they told her they didn't have a public phone. She walked down the street to the nearest phone booth down by the alley to call her roommate Shirell. She returned back to the hotel and stood by the lobby to wait for her friend. She picked her up from the hotel. Shirell asked her, "Who was that man who was watching you? Nadia, you need to be careful being out alone at night."

"I don't know who he is, but I noticed him too. The man stood there watching me walk away from the hotel."

They went back to the spot where her car was located and looked for her keys. Her keys were near her tires. This was strange because she checked around the entire car and nothing was on the ground. This was a mystery to her. Her main key to her car was the only key from her keychain missing. When she got out of her car to throw away her bathrobe into the garbage can was when it went missing. She threw it away because it had been around Boris's home. In witchcraft, they use personal items such as a lock of hair or something that belongs to you to cast their spell. Her robe had been in possession of Boris for many months. She didn't want to take the chance of keeping it in her vehicle. When she got rid of it, the demon got rid of her car key. Immediately after that, Shirell took her to the hospital so she could rest and calm down. She checked into the hospital around two thirty in the morning, and they gave her a bed. She was sitting down, and suddenly from out of nowhere, she could hear the sound of a chainsaw swinging back and forth underneath her hospital bed. She stomped her feet on the bed to let him know, "you devil! I'm tired of you running after me." It stopped for a short period of time. It continued on from a distance. It felt like pure terror at that moment because the sound was getting closer to her. She didn't scream or say anything. Something came over her. The more distressed she seemed to be, the more he would come to terrorize her. It seems to subside when she showed no emotions. It had no pity for her. She couldn't see this entity, but she knew it was there. It was pure evil she was dealing with. She could hear him gunning up the chainsaw in the middle of the hospital. He would move closer to her every time she felt frightened.

Before her examination took place, she waited patiently behind the portable curtain for the doctor. She remembered the curtain had a printed flock of owls on it. Her memory was sort of foggy, but she was sure of what she saw. The owls had human faces on it. They were shown to her for a reason. They wanted her to imitate the faces she had seen on the curtain. She believed it had something to do with some sort of initiation. They were trying to convert her over into their organization. They wanted her to belong to the black jacket society. It's a society who wears black to symbolize Satan. This is the same organization who had tried to put her to sleep or, even worse, harm her. The faces that she saw were expressions such as grimacing and anger, sneering and of being clever, sneaky, etc. She couldn't remember all the other images. There were more. She tried to mimic the images out of fear because she needed help from them. She knew she didn't pass the test because the doctor came in and was looking at her viciously. She didn't pass because she wasn't evil or cunning enough. This test was given to her to measure evil in her facial expressions. She didn't want any part of them anyhow. She just wanted a safe place to go. It looked really strange on that floor that night. She saw people snoring in deep sleep. When she left the hospital, she was also in a deep sleep. The nurse gave her a medication that made her hands and feet tingle and body ache. The medication had made her feel as if she were going to pass out. They must have given her something really hardcore. She was unable to keep her eyes open after that to see what was happening to her. She went home after treatment, and when she returned to her place, she saw the same umbrella sitting behind the coatrack. She threw it away down by the alley, and no one saw her doing it. She didn't know how it got back into her home or who returned it to her. It was so eerie to see that same umbrella again.

After being released from the hospital, her life began to change. It was peaceful again—all the negative energy subsided and went afar. She returned to her place of employment and resumed all things as usual. She took off a few months from work to relax her mind. It kept her from worrying about her ordeal. She walked inside of the copy room, and a couple of women began to talk. They muttered, "November will be here next week, and this is the month they return for her." Nadia was appalled. However, she ignored them as if she didn't hear anything. They watched for her reaction, but she remained calm. Nadia knew why they said it, and she was ready for the calamity to commence.

Nadia heard the voice of a woman and a man outside her home. It mumbled, "don't look outside your window." She stood motionless inside of her living room. She could hear some activity down the hall inside of her bedroom. A heavy force sat on her bed with great strength, and began to breathe deeply. The woman said, "don't go in that room, or else he'll eat you." It frightened Nadia so much she sat down on her couch, and she could feel this thing moving inside of her body. She screamed. It began to make a tapping sound against the couch. She saw a small colorless orb moving around in her living room. The demonic voice started screaming, saying, "He's going to eat you. Go to her front door and see if it is locked." Nadia had a hunch that they were going to drag her out of her own house by her ankles. Shriell, was in the other room. She heard Nadia yelling for dear life. She came into the living room and helped her. She called her close friend to come see about her. Laura came to pick Nadia up to take her to her home. The demons instantly left the house. She told her friend Laura what had happened. Laura invited her to come over to stay at her place. Upon coming to her house, Nadia saw a ghost entering through Laura's front window. It was a man. He stood about six feet tall. He entered through the glass. She shouted, "They're here. They followed us here. Take me back home please. I would rather be at my own place." Laura didn't see what Nadia saw. She drove her back home and pulled up in her driveway. Before Nadia could get to her front door, a pack of black hellhounds were chasing her. As she was running to her apartment, she turned back to see where they were. They had disappeared. She knew that the demons were trying to make her lose her mind. It is said that the devil himself sends his black hellhounds to drag a person's soul to hell. She thought that she would be okay at home. She stayed home and rested and prepared herself a meal. It started again. She could hear a man on the side of her house saying, "She is still hot." There was something unusual going on with her legs. She began to look down at her legs and saw that her lower limbs were contorted. She was aghast. She straightened out her legs and walked to her front porch. She yelled, "Get out of here, you bastards." Then she said, roughly glowering, "Go back to hell were you belong. Leave me alone. Get the hell out of here you devil." The demons gathered around her home, tapping at her windows. Nadia couldn't take it anymore. She called the police and went back to the hospital.

The entities followed her to the hospital. One of the demons appeared before her in a furry red rabbit suit with huge red glowing eyes. It wiggled his hand at her. She was in the emergency room on a gurney facing the front door. She could see it all. A security guard was on duty observing her. He was in charge of watching her that night. He was laughing when she complained about them harassing her. The fiend was verbally communicating with her as the doors opened and closed. He called her a bitch and a cunt. It was very loud. She looked to see if the guard was going to do anything about it, but he didn't. It spoke to her. He said, "you better not leave this hospital, or we'll get you." It was able to read her mind. In her mind, she thought about John, and the fiend verbally stated, yes he's one of us to. She figured it meant he was affiliated with this demonic group. She glanced over at the guard and wondered why he didn't get up to investigate. The demon continued to communicate with her. He said that he was going to go after her friend because she was getting paid for sex. The security guard sneered. When she saw him do that, she knew he could hear everything. She wanted to confront him, but it was not going to help the situation. It was unusual that he didn't get up or say anything about the noise or how many times the door opened or shut. She knew it had something to do with the conspiracy.

She tried earnestly not to look outside the exit doors where they stood. She pretended that she couldn't see or hear them because her stress level had reached its peak. With her peripheral vision, she saw a nurse standing in the hallway, staring at her with an evil eye. She made her feel uneasy. She got up and walked towards the front exit door, and the guard stopped her. Nadia uttered, I need to use the bathroom. The guard sternly said, "you can't use this one. Go to the one down the hall." Nadia walked to the second bathroom and went inside. She was given a hospital gown to put on, and she began to get undressed. She heard a voice as she was changing her clothes. He said, "You don't know how to put on the hospital gown correctly, and you don't have on any girly panties." Nadia replied, "You can go to hell," and she stormed out of the bathroom. She thought to herself, "What kind of demon is this?" She returned to her gurney that was in the middle of the hallway. She asked, "Nurse, could I please move further down the hall because of the cold air. These demon people are outside are harassing me."

The nurse asked, "what demon people?"

"There are men and women outside harassing me."

The nurse uttered, "sure, I will move you."

She moved, and she could still hear them in one of the bedrooms talking. They were penetrating through the walls trying to get to her. She was about to have a nervous breakdown, but somehow she held herself together and didn't snap and lose her mind.

The nurse gave her a sedative to make her relax. She lay on the gurney with her eyes closed, and she heard a man say, "Take this medication or else you're coming with me." She took the medication out of fear. A few minutes later, she spewed out something that looked like a clay man. She could not believe what had just happened. She didn't save it to show it to the staff or have it examined. They tortured her for hours. A woman who was sitting next to her was in a great deal of pain. She looked at Nadia, and immediately after that, the building became icy cold. She heard the doctors saying they felt it too.

Nadia kept her eyes closed most of the night because the tension was great. However, she peeked a bit outside the exit doors and saw something moving really fast like a train. It continuously ran parallel to the front entrance door. It seemed unusual to be there. It was there for several seconds. She remembered seeing it at her apartment too. It looked like something they used to travel in and take you away in. She didn't take lightly what she saw. They were near the exit door for several hours. The demonic woman yelled, "She insane, she insane." They wanted her to break down. She was scared out of her mind of what they were going to do to her. She was glad that they didn't carry her away. Staff was all over the place that night. It looked chaotic. It was like nothing she had ever seen before. Nadia closed her eyes, and the incubus was next to her. She didn't want to look at it. It had whiskers; it touched her face. She couldn't get herself to open her eyes. His face was next to her face. Had she opened her eyes, she would've seen a hellish fiend. She probably wouldn't have ever been the same. She wasn't strong enough to handle it. The demonic woman bellowed, you better scream. Nadia begins to scream, she said you better scream louder or else I'll cut out your tongue. A man uttered, "you're coming with me." Nadia was in tears. She was yelling and screaming for her life. A nurse came to her and asked, "why are you screaming?" She couldn't talk about it or open her eyes.

When her eyes were tightly closed, she could see virtual images of an animated woman falling down into a deep elongated pit. When she reached the bottom, she tried to climb out of it. She was struggling to get out of it. They stated, "Look at her. She's trying to climb out the pit, but she can't." Nadia opened up her eyes and yelled, "what are you doing to me?" She closed her eyes again. The woman was walking in a field, and she was very shapely and curvaceous. When she walked, it was sexual and sensual. Nadia could alter her movements with her mind. Nadia was able to make her walk like a respectable woman. They were judging, condemning, and evaluating her. They accused her of lascivious acts. She felt like they were pressuring her to tone it down, or they would destroy her. She opened her eyes, and she looked around the hospital. When she shut her eyes again, she could see herself in a red Ferrari speeding down a deserted highway at night with fire alongside the road. Again when she reopened her eyes, everything returned back to normal. Nadia shouted, "why am I seeing all of these weird hallucinations?" Nadia looked and was amazed, she saw another vision. It was several enormous burning holy crosses right before her eyes. They were heading towards her hospital bed. Staff asked, "does he still care for her?" Nadia's first inclination was am I condemned? A nurse came over to her bed, and Nadia told her that she was seeing things. The nurse told her that she would go and get her some medication. Nadia said, "I don't need any medication. These things are not in my head."

A visitor was sitting in one of the rooms watching her the whole time she was there. She seemed to have compassion for Nadia. She knew what she was going through but couldn't help her. Nadia felt helpless, and nobody was there to step in and help her. These monsters were above the law. While on the gurney, they pulled her down the hallway, and they put her inside a quiet room that looked like a nursery. It had no babies in the room, but they put her in there because she was yelling in the hallways. The demons were next to her. She couldn't open her eyes anymore, and she felt as if she was on a carnival ride in that room. Her memory of this room is a little foggy, but she remembered seeing all sort of colors and kiddy imagery. She didn't know the purpose of it, but she was spinning and twirling around in the room. It was a very bright room with a corpse inside of it. She was brave enough to peek at the corpse that was about four feet from her. She was horrified when she saw it. She could see the guard looking through the window at her, watching her every movement. She soon blacked out from the medication and fell asleep. The demons were most likely caught on film that night. The cameras were located on the outside of the building, and they were constantly filming the area where the demons stood.

Nadia was transferred to a psychiatric hospital. They took her across town to another ward. She stayed there for about one week. She shared her room with three other roommates. The food was horrible. While in the hospital, she had a discussion with her Psychologist. He had asked her, "how are the voices?" She told him that they came over to her window and they talk to her. He said, "Do you realize that they're not real and that they're just in your head?" This troubled her because she knew they were real and not in her head. "What did they say to you?"

"If I tried to figure out what they are saying, I believe this gives them the opportunity to get closer to me and harm me."

He said, "they can't harm you."

She looked at him and thought to herself, "you're a fool." They can harm you. These fiends have a way of tricking you into believing them. If you believe what they are saying, it gives them access to get close to you and harm you. They will say 'she bought it,' 'she believes it,' and they will get closer to me." It felt like déjà vu to her again. The Psychologist explained to her how they initiate. He asked, "Can you can hear them in a far distance or at a close range?" "How could he have possibly known, this information?" She wondered.

She muttered, "they come to me exactly how you explained it. I can hear them shouting in a far distance, and then they come to me at a close range. If I put my energy into listening to them, they come to my window. They tell me really horrible stuff.

"What did they say?"

"I will not go there because it's so devastating. I can't even talk about it."

"I'm here for you if you want to share that information at another time." He then asked, "what did you do when you heard the voices?"

She explained, "The very moment they began to try to harass me, I took a shower, and when I came back to my room, they were gone. It has something to do with me cleansing with water. I believe this is why they left." They ended their consultation and agreed to meet again.

Friday morning she attended group therapy. Dr. Robin Petersburg walked into the room and sat down in her chair. She flung her curly red hair to the side and began to look at the clock. She muttered, "It's 10:00 a.m. Let's begin. I want everyone to discuss what they did this week and share something special about yourself."

There were about twenty people sitting in the circle. Nadia was the third person to be asked to speak. As she looked up at her and looked her into her eyes to talk, she felt faint and very weak. Dr. Petersburg's eyes were hypnotic. She asked Nadia, "how are you feeling today?" Her thought was, "what did you just do to me.?" I know what you are! Your one of those demons," and she knew right at that instant not to look into her eyes again. Nadia knew who she was dealing with. She didn't call her out on what she did to her during group meeting. If she would've confronted her there, she was sure she would've denied it and said, "I don't know what you're talking about." "Or it's all in your head." They probably would have asked her to leave the group. Nadia thought about saying something to her. But she was afraid to do so. She wanted to expose her. It all happened so quickly; she was not prepared for it. Frankly, she was unable to defend herself. She nearly passed out. Nadia acted as if nothing happened to her and it didn't have an effect on her. She participated in group therapy, knowing she had done this to her. She fled the room after it was time to break and did not return back that day. They called her home and asked why she left the group early. She told them she left early because she felt ill and thought, "What do these people think? They could use their black magic against me willingly?" She went home in a panic and called Maleya. She told her that she was in group therapy, and when it was time for her to talk, she looked in Dr. Petersburg's eyes and she felt faint. I don't know why she did that to me. If she had the opportunity, she would've done something a lot worse."

Nadia explained to Maleya I'm a Christian woman who believes in the Bible. She believes that some people are here to do Satan's work. In Revelation 12:9, it says, "And the great dragon was cast out, that old serpent, called the Devil, and Satan, which deceived the whole world he was cast out into the earth, and his angels were cast out with him." They were here to do the work of the devil. It's a battle here on earth for God's children. The devil is a liar and a tempter. She is a fighter and will not give up. She will not let them get her down anymore. She is no longer timid. She's a stronger woman now. This has made her grow. It has made her tough as nails. She is no longer afraid of them. There is a reason for everything. This is a trial to measure her faith. The Lord is watching over her. He is molding and shaping her. She has forgiven the people who tried to harm her; Her faith is renewed. She will not let go of her hope of peace and tranquility. She has been through many obstacles. However, she is going to stay strong and will not be moved in her faith. Her prayers will not go unanswered. The Lord has strengthened her to go on every day.

CHAPTER 5

She left her job as a Laboratory Assistant. The problem was affecting her there too. She never told anyone there that she was having any problems. Someone had indirectly told her that they were coming for her. She believed it to be true because the entity did come that year to torment her. She heard someone say, if she said hi more than three times a day, she would be finished, and the doors to the netherworlds would open up and come finish her. Another person said as he was passing by her, "they won't destroy you." He knew what she was going through and wanted to warn her.

In the past, she was a happy-go-lucky person. She was an ordinary woman who loved life. She didn't have all the answers to why this was happening to her. She was from a small town in, California. As a child, she loved reading novels and competing with the other children to see who would finish first. In her teenage years, she was very active. She was a pitcher for an all-girls softball league. She pitched ball very well. Before she started playing ball, her team was in last place. They were able to attain third place after she arrived. She also achieved a yellow belt in karate. Those were the days she missed—the summertime when she used to catch tadpoles at the creek. She would make money selling them to classmates. She enjoyed family vacations to national parks. When she was nineteen years old, she cruised to Hawaii, with her friend, Maleya. They stayed their three nights and one day. They met several single people and mingled with them. During their vacation they danced and partied all night long. They drank blue tropical drinks and ate steak and lobster. In her twenties, she became a Laboratory Assistant and studied Microbiology. When she was twenty-one, she flew to Las Vegas in the summer with her friend to celebrate her birthday. Since the haunting has taken place, it has stripped her of her happiness. She has tried to seek out professional help for her problems, but nothing seemed to work. This frustrated her. It has made her very tensed and under a lot of pressure. She was a caring and nurturing person in the past. She enjoyed helping people. She always goes out of her way to help people who were in need. She loves animals and nature. When she was a young girl, she was passionate about animals. She took in a guinea pig from middle school. She was the first student in line to get him. She named him Guinea, and she was crazy about him. When he died, she buried him in a shoe box with her photo inside it. The next year, she got a rabbit and named him Floppy. When he would break loose, she would catch him, and he would give her a good buck. Her family used to raise ducks and chickens. She was the second eldest child in the family. She came from a hardworking lineage. They always had just enough to make it. They never went without clothes or food. She was a happy child growing up. Spiritually, she was well balanced. She knew that there was a reason for everything. "What I'm going through is temporary," she told herself. She knew there'd be light at the end of the tunnel. However, she has support from friends and family. She still thought that they didn't quite understand what she had been going through. She didn't think they believed her. Knowing this bothered her. They grew up with her, so how was it possible that they didn't believe her? They had a difficult time believing that those things were possible. They didn't want to believe her because they feared the unknown. They knew what she told them was true and was factual. They still told her that it was all in her head and that she needed to take her medication. This offended her, and she couldn't believe that they didn't take her word seriously. However, she still stood strong and believed in herself even though nobody else did. No one could change her mind. She is willing to stand alone if necessary.

She had been plagued by this situation for three years. She wanted to belong to a church to call it her own. Church is good for the soul, and it has made her feel protected. She is a believer in faith. She was raised in the church as a child, and her grandfather was a deacon. She enjoyed doing and hearing the word of God. Last year she got baptized in her friend's church. She met him at a grocery store. He was handing out innovations to his church. They kept in touch with each other for over ten years. He was a role model to her. He helped the homeless and the brokenhearted. He would give his right arm for others.

Nadia is currently in a relationship and he doesn't know her past. She's not sure if she wants to tell him. She's been dating him for four months, and she met him at college. She was walking to her classroom, and he asked for her name. He replied, "I'm Fredrick. It's a pleasure to meet you." She instantly could tell that he was a genuine guy.

She said, "It's nice to meet you too, Fredrick."

He smiled and asked her, "what are your interest and goals.?"

"I want to be a Biologist, and someday travel the world."

"You're not asking for much, Nadia. My plans are to become a Physician Assistant. I want to help the poor and disadvantaged. Your health is the most important aspect of your life." "You're absolutely right, Fredrick. You are in the right field. It's good to hear that there are still honest and good people out here."

"Could I walk you to your class?" he asked.

"Sure. It's just right over there."

He asked her, "Hey, is it possible we could exchange telephone numbers?"

"Of course we can."

She gave him the phone number, and he replied, "I will definitely be calling you."

She smiled and said, "Good-bye, Fredrick."

He wiggled his fingers and said, "bye now."

She entered the classroom with a huge smile on her face. Her classmate, Amber asked her, "what's the huge grin on your face all about?"

"What why, Amber?"

"Because, I know you. You're usually serious when I see you."

She said, "I look serious! Really? Well, if you really must know, I just met Fredrick. He walked me to class. We exchanged telephone numbers."

"See, I knew it. You had that look on your face."

"I don't know what will happen between him and I but it's always nice to meet a gentleman."

A week later she received a phone message from Fredrick. She was working and was busy, and she missed his phone call. He had left a message saying, "Hi, Nadia, this is Fredrick. I met you at school a week ago. Would you call me back please when you get a chance? I would like to take you out this weekend if that is okay with you. Call me soon."

She called him back as soon as she heard the message. He picked up his phone instantly and he said, "Fredrick speaking."

"Hi Fredrick, I just got your message, and I'm returning your phone call. What's up?"

"Well, I just wanted to know if maybe you'll let me take you somewhere special this weekend."

She asked, "what do you have in mind?"

"Have you ever been to a wine tasting gallery?"

She said, "No. It sounds really nice."

He answered, "well, you're a nice girl, and I would like to take you to some nice places." She responded, "well, thank you."

He muttered, "you're welcome." I will pick you up twelve noon Saturday."
"I'll be waiting, Fredrick. Good-bye."

He picked her up at exactly twelve noon. She dressed plainly; she wore a pair of jeans and a flowing long sleeve top with a flat pair of sandals. He wore Jeans pants and a button up shirt. They rode on the wine train and ate a gourmet lunch. He ordered a steak, and Nadia ordered lobster. They toured the vineyards and sampled the wines. The scenery was gorgeous. She told him that he had very good taste, and she enjoyed his company. They later took a walk in town near the downtown waterfront. They watched the boats sail as couples held hands. He asked her, "What are you looking for in a man?"

"Most importantly, trust. Without it you have nothing. Second, I want a commitment. I don't want a man who runs around. If my man wants to see other people, all he has to do is just let me know. I don't like to be deceived. What are you looking for in a woman?"

"What I actually love is when a woman can trust and believe in me. I want to know that she will be on my side through the good and bad times."

"Fredrick, I can understand where you're coming from. Everyone goes through rough times, and when situations arises, it's comforting knowing that you have someone standing by your side."

"Nadia, it sounds like we have a connection."

He reached out to her and gave her a comforting hug. They continued walking down the pathway.

He later drove her home. He asked, "So how did I do on the first date?"

"Well, as a matter of fact, you're a winner."

"Oh yeah, you think so? Well, you're easy on the eyes and fun to be around. I would love to take you out again. It's been a pleasure spending time with you, Nadia. So tell me what is your schedule like, Nadia"?

"I work Monday through Friday. I'm a part-time student. I go to school on Mondays and Wednesdays." Nadia asked, "What does your schedule look like?"

"I have to work next weekend, but I will give you a call early next week, Nadia. I would like to spend more time with you."

"I would love that, Fredrick. Just let me know when. I'm usually not busy on the weekends."

He walked her to her door and kissed her on the cheek. She looked into his eyes and said, "I had a wonderful time today. I would like to do it again."

He reached for her chin and gently tilted it upward and said, "Yes, I definitely want to spend more time with you. Fredrick, thank you for everything. Call me."

She opens her front door, and he turned her around and reached out for her hand. He kissed it and he began to walk away. "Fredrick, would you care to join me for a while? I have some chilled wine in the refrigerator."

Raising his eyebrow, he said, "yes, of course."

He walked inside and sat on the living room sofa. She walked into the kitchen and grabbed two chilled wine glasses that were in the freezer. "Fredrick, please come inside the kitchen. Would you please reach for the cork screw in the drawer near the sink and open the bottle of wine?"

"It will be my pleasure doing so." He popped open the wine and poured the wine into the wine glasses. He announces, "let's toast, Nadia."

She said, "Okay, I will have to say, all our dreams will soon come to a reality; and even though we just met, I'm impressed and fascinated with how well you have treated me. No other man has taken out the time to show me the finer things in life. I appreciate that about you."

He let out a big laugh, and said, "I have a lot more things I want to show you. Give me the chance to show you that I'm really here for you."

They toasted and took a sip of their wine. He stroked her hair and put it behind her ear. She felt a pulsating sensation go through her body. They walked over to the couch, and he held her. He whispered gently in her ear, "You are well worth the wait. I must go now. I don't want to rush you into anything. I will come back another time."

She totally understood where he was coming from. She respected him for that. She walked him to his car, and they kissed. He drove off and went home. She took off her jeans and sandals and rubbed her feet. She reached for the telephone and called Maleya. "Girl, I just had the best time of my life with Fredrick."

She said, "Fredrick? You got to tell me all about him."

"I met him in college. We exchanged phone numbers, and he walked me to my classroom. We just made it back from a long walk at the waterfront. We also went wine tasting and rode on the train. We had a wonderful time together. He is a single man without kids."

Maleya said, "Your lucky to have found him. "Yes, girl, I did. I think he is a keeper. He asked me what I was looking for in a man. I told him I wanted an honest and loyal guy. I was glad to hear that he wanted a woman who could trust him and be by his side. We plan to go out again in the next couple of weeks. I'm looking forward to meeting with him again. He whispered in my ear telling me that he didn't want to rush me into anything. How many men can say that? I'm glad we didn't do anything, girl, because I don't want him to think that I'm a loose woman."

"Yes, girl, sounds like a good idea. Just let me know how things work out for you guys."

"I will."

"Girl, I'm about to run me some bath water, and I will call you later."

"Okay, talk to you later, Maleya. Bye."

CHAPTER 6

Nadia was delighted to have finally met the man of her dreams. He was kind and honest. He had no bad intentions that she knew of. She didn't have to worry about him trying to harm her. She made sure that she didn't run into a weirdo. They kept in touch with each other and went out on several dates. She met with his family. His parents were still married for over twenty-five years. They lived in California. They dated for over one year, and he proposed to her. She wasn't ready for marriage. She had a lot of baggage underneath her belt. She told him that she wanted to continue the relationship with him. However, she needed to spend more time with him in order to make her decision. She still hadn't told him about the haunting. She was afraid that he would run away and she would lose him. She didn't want him to think that she was crazy. This is the first assumption that people have when these sorts of things occurs.

Months later, she finally got the nerve to tell him that she had been having trouble with her ex-boyfriend and that he may have put a hex on her. He believed her instantly and asked her why she didn't tell him earlier. She told him that she thought that he would've thought she was out of touch with reality. She let him know that it felt good knowing that somebody believed her and wanted to protect her. She felt more confident about herself and coped with the stress. He told her that he had her back and he will be there for her in her time of need. He wanted to get to the source of this problem. He knew every detail about her ordeal. Nadia believed that the demons were not finished with her. She thought that they would come again to seek her out and destroy her. They didn't come for her last year, but they did in November and December two years ago. Nadia rationale is that maybe they didn't come back for her last year because she had gotten baptized in water and received holy water from Pastor Rick. He came to bless her home last year. She sprayed the holy water that she received from him around her home to keep them away.

She was free of the negative spirits. She have been using this method in her home frequently. "Fredrick, it's getting close to the end of the year, and I will invite Pastor Rick over to come and bless my home again."

"Whatever it takes to bring ease to your mind, I'm comfortable with, Nadia."

She was in traffic the follow day, Nadia ran into John in traffic. He blew his horn and waved at her and shouted, "pull over. I want to talk to you." He told her, "I know that I was a jerk in the past, and I apologize for what I did to you. I really do care for you, and I want you to know I miss you." Let's get together and start up a friendship again. She told John that she was in a serious relationship with Fredrick, and she didn't think that it would be appropriate to see one another. He pressured her to exchange telephone numbers with him so that he could talk to her. He wanted to know what was going on in her life. He muttered, "I got married, and we've got a divorce." Nadia asked him what happened. He told her that it didn't work out for them. Nadia gave in to him. She began to let him in on her personal life. Nadia told John everything about the haunting and the medication her doctor prescribed for her to take. He didn't believe that she was actually being tormented by a demon. He told her that she must keep taking her medication before something more drastic happens to her. He told her that her situation sounded minor. She thought to herself, "why would I go through something more drastic if I stop my medication?" Nadia explained to him that she didn't have a problem. She just didn't know what was going on. If she was delusional, she would be having these sorts of issues on a daily basis. There are many times that she doesn't take her medications, and nothing happens to her state of mind. She discussed with him that this was the third year that they came for her. The first year they had come to her residence to scare her with the chainsaws. She told him that it's hard to fight what you don't understand. "They came to arduously pressure me, and they tried to make me sick. They try to make you harm yourself first without putting hands on you. When I was in my apartment, I wanted to get away really bad. If it wasn't for my roommate stopping me, I could've fallen down the stairs and broken my leg or, even worse, injured myself trying to get away. Know this. They're tricky if you're in a crazed state of mind. When you're afraid, anything is possible. It's important to tell someone and never be alone. My friend Pastor Rick always tells me to read my bible for protection. They're fallen angels doing the deeds of the devil. They are here for a reason. I know what happened to me, and I know what I saw. It can happen to anybody. I didn't put this curse on myself. I got involved with the wrong person, and he's been trying to harm me ever since. "John, in the first year of the haunting, I would frequently hear many things." Many times I would hear the sound of drums beating and horn blowing before the fiends would arrive to my home. They do this to let me know they're coming with great power and authority. It wasn't my neighbors' kids playing the drums or blowing the horn because it happened again when I moved to my new place. They do it to make their presence known. I moved three times since the haunting has taken place. It has stripped me of my happiness."

He laughed and said, "you think just because you hear a horn blowing and drums beating, this means that they are coming for you? Please, Nadia, don't believe that. It's simply children around your neighborhood practicing with their instruments."

Nadia muttered, "I have been made a believer in the mystery of the unknown. I'm frustrated with my situation. I'm under a lot of emotional turmoil and stress. I think about seeking help from a paranormal team. But I often think that I would become the laughingstock of the neighborhood or get ridiculed."

He stated, "Don't go there, Nadia. Don't do it."

She told him, "I want to ask a priest to come and cleanse and bless my home. I figured it would be difficult for me to prove my case; that I'm actually being tormented by a demon and not suffering from a mental illness, especially after my prior hospitalization. I felt as though others would not take me seriously, and they might say I must've lost my mind. I had to take matters into my own hands and brought some white protection candles and a bundle of sage and lit them. The smell of the air was thick. The aroma was intense. While the sage was burning, I read Psalm 23. I recited, 'let no negative spirits come into this place.' I walked into all the bedrooms and let the smoke from the sage penetrate the four corners of the walls. I used this method to run off the negative energy. I waited each year for them to come and attack me. It is the month of November now."

"Nadia, I'm telling you, it's all in your head. Don't believe it. It's true your mind is playing tricks on you."

"John, I hear you, but I must go home. I will talk to you later."

She knew he had given her some fallacious advice. She purchased several security cameras and placed them around her house so that she could capture the demonic activity. John told her that she was out of her mind and that she wasted her money on the cameras. He discouraged her. He told her that she needed to seek out professional help because she was getting out of control. She listened to what he had to say and said nothing more. She knew he was a deceiver. She questioned his accountability and didn't take him seriously. He was not a loyal or a true friend. However, her gut feeling was telling her that John might know something. She didn't have all the answer to why this was happening to her. How could he predict what will happen to her if she didn't take her medication? She stayed in touch with him because she knew that he had more information to tell her. She waited for him to slip up and give out clues. She hadn't informed Fredrick that she ran into him and they talked. She was sure that he would disapprove of them associating together, and he would become upset.

She was anxious to know what was going on around her, so she visited a psychic reader and had a reading done. The medium hit the nail right on the head. She told her that the darkness was following her and that Nadia didn't need a psychic to tell her that because she already knew it herself. She showed her the hand of cards that the fortune-teller dealt her, and it was indeed atrocious. The devil's card appeared in the pile of cards right before her eyes. It was a dreadful sight. The psychic medium told her that she was able to do a chakra cleansing for her for the price of $1,500 dollars. The cleansing will free her from the curse, and through mediation she will be able to tell her who is responsible for cursing her. The psychic stated, "the cleansing clears the spirit, mind, and body. The Chakra is a seven wheel of energy system. The crown, which is located at the top of your head; it includes the hips, legs, lower back, and; the sacral, the third eye cleansing includes intuition and the solar plexus, which is in your gut. These areas can become out of balance, and I am able to help you to regain your stability." I can also forebode your future. Nadia stated, wow you can predict what I will be doing in the future? The psychic said, yes, of course I can, are you prepared to hear what I'm going to tell you? Nadia hesitated; right now I don't think I want to know my future. How much will you charge me for my reading?
Nadia mumbled, "I can't afford it at this time."
"You shouldn't let the curse go on like that any longer because it is affecting your health," the psychic told her. "It has drained you of your energy and freedom. Am I right?"
Nadia responded, "you're absolutely right." It has a tremendous effect over me, and I'm going crazy."
"Nadia, you need a qualified person like myself to help you. You shouldn't try to remove it yourself because you don't know what you're dealing with."
Nadia was listening to her very carefully and told her that she would call her back soon with her decision. Nadia was perplexed she never heard of these types of cleansing before. It was too much information to comprehend. She didn't know how she was going to afford the cleansing. She knew she needed it for her protection. It was getting closer to the time that the haunting all began.

She hired a private investigator to follow Boris. She found out that he goes to a candle store on a weekly basis and buys items from a woman who sells voodoo dolls out of her botanical spiritual shop. They say birds of a feather flock together. He also has a friend named Seth Sean who works as a warlock. He has a website for casting returned love spells and put curses on people for money. If they were involved in those sorts of activities, then it is possible he is doing it as well. They had come into her home and taken on the form of spirits and ghouls to torment her. It may seem like its far-fetched, but it is real. She still couldn't believe what had happened to her in the past. However, it upset her that those people have gotten away with it, running her down like some sort of wild animal. She's not going to put up with it any longer. She will do whatever it takes to seek justice. She will do whatever it takes to defend herself. She was waiting for the moment to come when she could confront her diabolical tormentor. She is no longer afraid of him. She wanted to tell him her mind. But it may infuriate him even more, or worse, it may even open up the doors and unleash the unholy upon her. The universe is full of mysteries, and nothing is impossible.

CHAPTER 7

She went to a doctor's visit, and she was sitting in the waiting room. Across from her was an empty chair, something was doodling on the empty chair. It drew different types of patterns and shapes on it. It didn't frighten her at that time; she just looked at it in amazement. When she was called into the examination room, she saw something else that was strange. She saw a ghostly shadow on the wall. It was clear in color and moved like running water. She thought that they had taken her soul. Something suspicious was going on in there. They may have been doing some sort of experiment on her. "Why is it that whenever she is admitted there, she could see all sort of unexplainable things?" she thought. After leaving the hospital examination room, she went to pick up her prescriptions. The clerk laughed and stated, "It's all in your head. It will be okay." Another man mentioned something like, "could you resist the devil?" Nadia didn't want to sound like a mental case that believed that aliens had come down and stolen her brain. Her point was that she was a normal person with no prior problems with the paranormal. She was trying to piece the clues together. She figured that she could assume that Boris was responsible for her torment because she had seen him in a vision. He was obviously involved with them. How can she protect herself against the gang of wolves? Nadia stated that she no longer wants to be a science project. She will take matter into her own hands and, if necessary, call the authority. It is difficult to prove a case of witchcraft, but she found evidence that his associates are involved in bizarre activities. Hopefully, the authority would take that into consideration.

She has been hospitalized twice because they were trying to harm her. They're also trying to sabotage her credibility. He has associates activity shows a motive. Nadia has a zero-tolerance towards being victimized. She has some information on him that may be to her advantage. She is trying to win this battle. They might have found a way to manipulate your brain so that you will have hallucinations. She will use her wits to outsmart them. The Lord is on her side, and he is looking down on her, encouraging her to continue on with her duties. They might've had the upper hand initially, but she will do whatever it takes to expel them. They messed with the wrong woman. The time is getting near for the anniversary of the haunting. But she has Fredrick by her side to protect her. She is recovering well after her hospitalization. She still has some issue with fear, but Fredrick has taken her underneath his wing, and he has helped her heart heal again. She is not alone; he will be there for her. She doesn't know what will happen next, but she is ready to move on with her life. She believes that they might not come back for her because she isn't afraid of them. They can't run after her anymore because she will not be backing down. They can torment her in her dreams at night but in the back of her mind she knows that she is a survivor. They don't come back for the strong they come back for the weak. She is a stronger woman. She has put on the whole armor of God and is ready to war. "In the name of Jesus, I will fear no evil. Amen," she prayed. It is now the first month of November. Fredrick and Nadia is waiting for them to appear. She's not sure if anything will happen again. Only time will tell, but so far it's been peaceful. Nothing has come out to spook her.

She has left her work again to get away from the stress. She spends a lot of time with family and friends. She is looking to return back to school to finish up her degree. She is still searching for a church to belong to. John continues to call her on a daily basis. He still thinks that she has a problem. He keeps telling her that she needs her medication. He also wants to be in a relationship with her. On a continuous basis, he asks her to come to his home. She has visited him once. He doesn't know that she is watching him and that she doesn't trust him. Fredrick is still in love with Nadia. She feels bad about visiting John behind his back. She will continue to be loyal to him. However, she feels the need to find out more information about her situation. She thinks if she can manipulate John into believing she is his friend, he will someday come clean about what has happened to her.

Nadia called Amy, and they talked about their relationships and careers. Amy is her close friend. She confides in her. "You know I've been keeping John around just to find out what he knows."

"Amy, I don't think you should do that because you may never find out a thing. You should just forget about what has happened to you and try to move on with your life. Please promise me that you will. I don't think that it will happen to you again."

"Amy, you're always straight forward. I think I will do that and not worry about my future. I will take it one day at a time. I don't want those negative thoughts to enter into my mind. This is the month of my horrifying ordeal. But so far, knock on wood, nothing has happened to me. Amy, I'm sort of anxious about it. If you were in my shoes what would you have done?"

"I'm not sure because it scares the heebie-jeebies out of me. Let's not go there anymore." "Sure, we can talk about others things."

"How do you feel about getting out of the house tonight? I cooked tacos."

"Girl, I will meet you. What time should I come?"

"You're welcome to come now if you want."

"Well, I'm sort of busy cleaning my house. I will be at your place at six o'clock. Save me a plate please."

Nadia headed to Amy's place. She handed her three turkey tacos. She reached in her refrigerator and pulled out three chilled beers. Amy man was in the living room watching the sporting channel. Nadia sat down at the dining room table and began eating. She muttered, "Nadia, you put your special touch into these tacos. You have to tell me the recipe."

Amy stated, "I'm glad you enjoyed them. I will show you how to make them the next time you stop by. I hope you enjoy your meal."

"Thank you, girl."

Amy uttered, "Nadia, what do you want to watch? My man is leaving to go to the store. Would you care for anything?"

"No, I'm fine. I'll just drink this cold beer. Do you have any action-packed movie or any drama flicks?"

"Yes, I do have something in mind. Just walk over to the entertainment center and pull out a movie of your choice."

Nadia stayed at her place overnight. She slept on the couch in the living room.

Nadia came home to an empty house the next morning. She felt a little bit uneasy about entering her home because of her paranoia. As she checked around the whole apartment, she entered into each bedroom. She suddenly heard something fall to the ground. It was her car keys. She found them in the middle of the floor. A weird feeling came over her. She couldn't explain why they fell down. She picked up her keys and ran out of the house. She went back to Amy's place to calm down.

She later came back home, and she could see the light on in the second floor bedroom. She was relieved that her roommate was home. She anxiously explained to her that she hung her keys on the key rack and somehow they fell down to the floor. Shirell said, "There's got to be a reasonable explanation for it. Maybe you didn't put on the hook correctly. You look really disheveled. Would you care to have some tea?"

Nadia took her up on her offer. They sat down, ate cookies, and drank lemon tea. She felt a bit better knowing that she had a shoulder to cry on. "I know I need to stop letting the little things bother me, Shirell. But, I don't want to become a paranoid schizophrenic. I know that it has a lot to do with my past. It's hard to let it go. I have been to group therapy for it, but nothing seemed to be helping me. How do I get over it, Shirell? Everything that happened to me in the past wasn't just my imagination working overtime. It happened to me three consecutive years. I was literally being brutally tormented by a group of individuals with an agenda. When that happened to me, it made me become paranoid, and this is the same month it all began."

"Nadia, I hear you, girl, loud and clear. Most of all stay strong and be prayerful. Maybe the last three years was the end of your ordeal. Don't let it consume you. I'm here. I will keep my eyes and ears open for you. Don't be secretive. If something does go on, let me know about it. I doubt that anything will happen. But if you hear anything, please yell out for help. I will be there for you."

"Shirell, I hope you're right. I hope this curse doesn't resurface. I was hoping that this year would be quiet for me. However, my nine-year-old cousin told me that he was standing on the stairwell, and he looked down into the living room, and he saw a little girl with a long white dress on. He said she had black hair and white skin. I asked who was she, and he told me that he didn't know who she was and that she looked like a ghost. He said she walked with her head slumped, walking slowing through the living room, and then she disappeared. When he told me this story, it sent chills down my spine. These are the first sightings of a ghost in my new home. It seems like they follow me wherever I go. I try to banish them, but they manage to come back. Two years ago, I heard the sound of a church bell inside of my car. It sounded like some sort of marriage was going to take place. I'm not sure what it meant." I asked a friend and she told me that these signs means destruction or they want to harm you.

Shirell uttered, "Nadia, nothing will happen to you. Don't believe your friend and kids make up stories. If I were you, I would let it go." I would, but it's happening again. Other people has witness it too. This is the anniversary month when it all begins. I don't know what's my fate, and the beginning of November is near." However, I do know this, whenever Boris and I paths seems to cross we collide. It seems like whenever we encounter a romantic union or interact with each other in some kind of way, strange things starts to happen. What I have recently discovered, is that when I was a young teenager.

I dabbled around with an Ouija Board. I never closed the portals to the gates of purgatory. I was an inexperienced child, who had no business messing with such an evil vile device. I was ignorant and foolish, It recently dawn on me that I did this when I was fifteen years of age. I can agree that many people especially young adults and teenagers do engage in these sorts of activities; not knowing the consequences of their actions. My subconscious mind has allowed me to somehow block out the memory of what I had did in my youth. During that time, I remember being in my backyard at that tender age. I saw what I will describe as a black non-human entity. It had no face or arms legs or torso. It was a mass of smoke. It spoke to me and said, "I would regret this day"; after playing around with the board. I made this board at home. "How did you make the board Shirell asked?" "I cut out a card board box into a square shaped figure, and then I added numbers and the alphabets with a felt tip pen. I then added a yes or no spot, like the original board to communicate with the other worlds. I also used a quarter as a planchette to communicate with the spirit world. It would move across the board like the ordinary game. Everything has started to unravel and make sense. I have lined up all my ducks in a roll. I have left the doors open to the other side for over a decade. I was told by a good friend that Boris's soul can leave his body at will. His spirit is invisible it can travel different dimension's. His physical body resides here on earth dwelling amongst human beings. During the anniversary month when it all begin; Boris's spirit comes to me seeking to invade and possess my soul. Now, that I have solved this imperative mystery, I have been instructed how to close the doors and never turn back to unlock them. The others seek my soul too, because I inviting them into my home unknowingly by doing so in my youth. I have received help from Pastor Rick. I was honest with him, I totally blank out, about what I did in my earlier days. My past has crept up on me. Evil forces has been watching me grow up through the years and blocking out the memory of what I have done. "Why and who was watching you aged through the years, Nadia? I think they had plans for me to become one of them. However, I choose another path. This is why they were evaluating me and watching me grow. Nadia, this seems so creepy and strange. "What are you going to do?" "How are you going to close the door, Nadia? I have begun by reading my scriptures aloud and prayer, sprinkling holy water around my home. I burned in a fire all of my gifts,' that I have received from Boris. I got rid of my bed we've slept in together, I moved again to another location. He tried to call me months later after we broke up. I have changed my number and I have lost all communication with him. I was told to never cross path again with him. If I do I would only be opening up the opportunity for him to do harm to me. The curse has been lifted and I have no reason to put myself in a situation like that again. I could be in dire jeopardy of losing my soul if I open the door again. I shall fear no evil. So far it's been nothing but peace and serenity in our home.

I have been through many obstacles. I remember it was valentine's day. I had just left Maleya's house. We had a few drinks and even partied a little bit. She didn't have anyone to spend the day with so I told her I would come over to her house and visit her. She had baked some sweetheart cupcakes for the occasion. I had been over there a few hours and I had left her home. Fredrick had to work late that night and the world as I know it had changed for me. I drove to an intersection and my life flashed right before my eyes. It was happening again to me, it was 11:00 pm and I knew evil was lurking. The stop sign had changed its appearance and it looked eerie. I looked at it with the corner of my eyes and it had changed into a creepy heart shaped figure with the letters l-o-v-e drawn across the stop sign board. My heart nearly fell to the floor. I couldn't take the harassment anymore. I put on my sunglasses and I drove away as fast as I could. I didn't want to look at it. It was so creepy and I wanted to avoid it. On my way home I saw a man trying to earnestly get my attention he wore a black bones and skull logo on his t-shirt. He wore all black and he stood there gazing at me near the freeway entrance. I nearly panic and I turned my head as quickly as I could. He tried to make eye contact with me. I wore dark shades to avoid eye contact. This sort of incident happened to me once before when I got out of the hospital. I had gotten out of the hospital and people where flagging me down on the streets. They wore those skeleton death doom shirts and everywhere I would go someone would show up in this logo on their shirt staring blankly at me. I think it's a cult thing and they were surely after me. I saw this guy immediately after I notice the stop sign with the heart on it. I put my head down and tried to look down at the road so that I don't make any contact with him. Or bring home any spirits with me. This entity force tried to attach itself to me. It wanted to scare me. I continued on my way home, and when I got home a strange man was standing in our parking lot. He was walking towards me and looking at me weird. I ran inside the house as fast as I could and locked the doors. I peeked outside my curtains and he was gone. I had gone to bed. The next morning I went to the same intersection where I saw the heart shaped stop sign and nothing was there on the stop sign. It had erased itself and return back to normal again. That freaked me out. I went back home and turned on my television, to watch a daytime program. I heard a man on the television say, "It's forbidden to watch, don't look!" I asked myself, "what is this man talking about?" I thought he was going to show something inappropriate. There were two women washing each other hair with shampoo. I look at them observing them washing each other hair. I felt weak and faint. I couldn't hardly get up off the couch and walk to the front door. I was going to faint. I panic and I started screaming and I turned off the television. That was the only thing I was able to do at this point. This evil force was now inside of my television controlling what I was watching. The people on the television show were odd. "Why would they say it was forbidden to watch and close your eyes?" They had warned the viewer's not to watch and to look away. I wonder if they knew that the devil was controlling their television program. Satan has power beyond any comprehension. Those people knew what they were doing. Shirell, do you thing I'm nuts?" "Nadia, how is it possible that people on the television can hurt you physically?" If that can happen it would shock the hell out of me. Shirell, I turned off the television and all of a sudden my body returned back to feeling normal again. I left my home afraid for my life. My comfort zone was gone. I couldn't even watch the television without it ruin my life. I went to Maleya's house, and I told her what I just explain to you. She thought of course, that I was losing my mind. She told me to relax it was only my imagination. She asked how was it possible for someone to look at the television and say it's forbidden to watch and then become dizzy and nearly faint. She laughed at me. She even told me to go and do a full checkup a physical because it could have been high blood pressure or even blood sugar problems. I agreed and went to the doctor and he ordered a full physical and did blood work up. He ordered a fasting blood sugar, potassium, cholesterol, complete blood count, and electrolytes test. I got back my results in about two weeks everything came back normal so that ruled out any possible medical conditions. I had told my doctor that I had been seeing and hearing things again and he told me that it was caused by my mental illness. He recommended me to increase and stay on my medications. I told the doctor that the television was talking to me. It had told me that it was forbidden to watch and that I should close my eyes. It warned me not to look, but to look away. The doctor again told me it wasn't real and that my mind was hallucinating. I know it had something to do with witchcraft and I was cursed by all these visions. The people on the television were after me and wanted to freak me out. After that experience, I felt like the world was closing in on me and if I made the wrong move I was doomed. I know damn well I'm not crazy because too many strange things have happened to me. I remember sitting in group therapy; I was in a deep fog. I saw the instructor's eyes open wide and they were pitched black, with no pupils. He had an inverted holy cross in the middle of his forehead. I was in a deep fog and I saw the instructors eyes open wide and they were pitched black with no pupils he had an inverted holy cross in the middle of his forehead. All of a sudden his eyes and face returned back to normal when he started talking. I was in a trance when I saw it. I remembered seeing it the next day. My mind had remembered it. I was in a fog when it happened because it's in my memory. However, I was in a deep trance when it happened. I had to pinch myself; I asked myself, did this really happen to me? I know it did because my mind keeps thinking about it over and over again. That same day I remember going home and hearing someone outside yelling and calling my name. I was watching television and it felt like it took on a life of it's own. The television was very hot like it was about to explode. I was watching a baby being born and the baby looked odd. It was red from head to toe. I got up to see what was going on outside, before I could focus in to see if this was a fictional show. I kept vaguely hearing someone calling my name. I looked outside the window and I didn't see anybody. I went back to watch the television and the picture of the baby was off the air before I could see it again. It looked like a red devil child. It scared the hell out of me out. I begin to call my friend, Maleya and I asked her, if I could come over to her house. The odd and bizarre occurrences scared me to death. It was strange seeing that weird looking baby being born and covered in red blood from head to toe. Suddenly I saw a swirl of black smoke twirling in a spiral coordination. It would fade in and out. I ran out of the house and called my doctor. I immediately went to the hospital to calm down. Later that night I went over to Maleya's house to spend the night. Before I walked up to her front door. I could hear a chainsaw gunning up violently in her backyard. She opens the door and I asked if she heard it. Of course, she didn't hear a sound. I came inside of her house and her wine glasses begin to chime, and bang against one another making a clinking sound. The wine glasses were hanging from the wet bar. She heard it but said it was a vibration for walking inside of the house. I feel asleep and I woke up with an ache in my belly. I had to vomit and had diarrhea so bad I thought I was going to fall to my knees and faint on the floor. She had to help me get on the couch and clean up the mess. The demon tried to suck the life out of me inside of her house. The next day I waited for you to return home. Before I step a foot inside of our apartment. I had a funny feeling come over me while watching television in my room. It felt like the television was trying to seduce me. I felt this warm and fuzzy feeling come all over my entire body. I rolled around my bed and I couldn't control the laughter and I felt getty and unusual. It didn't frighten me but I was amazed. It's sort of complicated to explain, but I was feeling like something came over me and I couldn't control what I was acting out. "Nadia, what are you trying to say?" I'm saying that I was watching a daytime program and my eyes felt heavy and my body felt like I was being seduced by the television. On another occasion I was being threatened by a man on television. The television had taken on a life of it's own. The man on the television had zoomed in on his face and body. It seemed like he was rapping and talking to me at the same time. His face got closer and closer to the camera on television. I got freaked out, I had to turn the television channel. It was like he was trying to intimidate me. I kept watching this man talk and rap on screen at the same time, while he was looking at me. His face was the only face that was showing on the screen he had an audience in the background. I could hear laughter; I was frightened to see this man face close up on the screen. I stood there and watched him. It felt like he could see me at home in my bedroom. "Nadia, are you serious?" "Believe me girl, I'm telling you the truth. I never experienced anything like that before." I don't want that to ever happen again. I was watching a romance story and a daytime program on television. A daytime program is what I was watching, when something jumped inside of my body and took over my emotions. It has something to do with the curse, I have been explaining to you. During astronomical event the lunar eclipse; something comes to invade my home, mind, body and soul. It comes to haunt me for a period of a month and a half. If I'm on the internet or watching television during the curse, it opens up doorways to hell. They use the internet and the television to get me to open up doors to the unknown. One incident was when I was on the internet and I saw a woman doing all sorts of bizarre jokes and I came across her video. It stated, "warning open door." As soon as I looked at her video, I woke up the next morning and the television went haywire. The television was talking about my life, my prior relationships and how I was being a noisy person. They said I never should have opened up the door. A woman stated, "oh my, what's that I want to see, should I open up this forbidden door?" She started laughing really hard and wicked. I stayed up all night and day just watching them talk about the choices that I had made and how they were going to take my soul. Nadia, that sounds weird and creepy let's talk about something else. "Now do you see what I'm going through, and how I had to figure out what in the hell was going on?" Also what doors I should keep closed and never opens again. When I get close to the month of the anniversary when it all begins I stay away from the internet and things warning me not to look because it's real I'm telling you. Whenever, I go through my trials from my curse. I can't even go to restaurants for takeout orders. I ordered food twice and they told me that they forgot my address, or my food is cold and they would have to put it back into the oven. It has control over the food I eat. One day, I went to get some food, and I had placed my order. My mind begins to race with thoughts. I had a feeling they could read my mind and they gave me bad food. They gave me the bad food, because they can read my bad thoughts. I had to feed it to the neighborhood dog because it tasted spoiled. Nadia, couldn't it have been just bad food they have given you? "Why would it have been bad, I don't think they would have served you bad food?" It's something the devil does when I go through my dark trials. Nadia, I still don't think it's the devil. Shirell, you should be a little bit more sensitive to the ideal that it happened to me. You should have known that I'm not crazy. If this were happening to you, you would want people to understand. People just don't believe in him because he not seen and he is in the shadows. That's the biggest misconception; people think it's a fairy tale when we talk about demons and spirits. It's always got to be where crazy or it's all in our head and or its not real. I'm here to say it is real and I do believe that I was chosen to go through hell because I open up that portal to the other side. I was sort of interested in weird stuff like the unknown as a teenager. That is why I made the Ouija board. When I made the board the forces of darkness was ready to attach itself to me. I was young when I done it. I didn't realize that was a way of it attaching itself to me. As soon as I closed the door to the other side now I've had no problems. I have been hexed for four years and I have written a book about it and I am pleased that I don't have to worry about it anymore. I don't think it will come around again because last year on the anniversary date it didn't resurface. I was on the internet and even watched television and I didn't see or hear anything unusual during the month that it resurfaces. I am so grateful to my friend pastor Rick. He was the one who told me to believe in what was happening to me. He informed me that it was not all in my head and showed me how to expel them. I go to church on a regular basis and I stay praying and avoid situations that could reopen the doors. These forces are very clever and there not easy to get rid of. I had to bathe in a ritual herb bath to pull off the negative energy that had attached itself to me. I was headed for destruction. These forces want you to believe that you're crazy but you're not. There in the shadows, and they want you to believe that there not real. Wanting you to take be lazy and not do anything about it. I was almost driven mad. I had little hope for myself. I thought I was out of my mind and nobody could do anything to help me. I figured everybody knew what was going on but me. A psychic told me that, I was under attack and I needed to get it off me. The curse would get to the point of where nobody could remove it. I would have to bathe seven days a week in a solution. I would have candles lit around my bathtub. Pastor Rick also did a séance for me and so far nothing has come to get me or take my soul. I know it worked, because around the lunar eclipse, when I was tormented, it was complicated. I have no problems with the supernatural now. I am now a happier person and Fredrick and I are getting married next year. Where planning on going to Hawaii with friends and family to get hitched. We are ready to make that move. Now that my life has be quiet and peaceful from all of those paranormal activities. Where even planning on having children in about a couple of years. He wants a boy and I want to have a girl. He wants to buy a home in California. I have finished up my schooling and know I'm looking for work. My life feels complete now. I'm ready to settle down and start a family. We have been looking for a home to purchase. He has finished school also. In about six more months my name will be changed to Mrs. Singleton. He adores me and I love him. We are inseparable. He is my better half. I can't see myself living without him. He knows about my past and he can appreciate my struggles and short comings.

He is the perfect man for me. I am so happy for once in my life. I can say that, all my worries and fears are behind me now. I am a complete person I feel whole again. Fredrick and I, go to the same church. Pastor Rick is planning to attend our wedding. I have my dress already. I feel good and I look great. I have four bridesmaids; it was a struggle to find the perfect dress, for the many different shapes. Everyone is pleased with the dress that they have purchased. My book will come out next year. I want to dedicate my book, to all the people who have struggled with the paranormal. I believe that there should be more help out there for others who are dealing with the paranormal. There are television shows that talks about it; I believe it goes on more than people care to believe. I wrote this book to give others a voice, and let people know that their not alone. It could happen to anyone, be careful not to dabble around with things were not supposed to. There's a rhyme and reason for everything. I just happen to be the one who wanted to go the extra mile unknowingly opening up the dimension to other worlds. I know there still out there, lurking waiting patiently, for the opportunity for others to do what I did. I will not be stuck on my past, I know I have beaten the odds, and prevail much. I hope that I could be an encouragement, to all those people whose voices went unheard. I could have easily lost my mind and been institutionalized or even swept away by the unknown forces. I wonder if I could have been one of those people, who were lost and had their soul swept away into the portal of hell. Nobody would have ever believed me and thought, I had lost my mind and gone astray. Sometimes you have to remember your past in order to do well in the future. I bring these things up to the surface, because I had done some bad things in my past. I thank my lord that I have been forgiven. Well, now that Fredrick has moved in with me things couldn't have been better. I can't believe that I was able to escape the dread and torture I endured. It was God's grace that saved me from my past. I had to figure out what I had done wrong and how to fix it on my own. They could have taken me away and killed me or even tortured me to death. I am a survivor, I can say that proudly at least. It seems so far fetch but I know the truth in my heart of hearts. "Nadia, now that you're feeling better, and you got rid of those so called demons, what's next?" "Shirell, all I can say is, I'm grateful." I will try to give back to others, and look for goodness in others. I don't have the answer to what's next, I will try to be happy with my fiancé, and hopefully grow old and tell my story to our grandkids. This is my testimony; if you haven't been through fiery trials, just count your blessings that you didn't have to go through them. I will stay positive and look at the world with new lens. I have grown wiser and with that wisdom; don't go looking for trouble, because trouble can easily find you.

The end

I have heard of several stories in my lifetime of bizarre things happening to random people. By sharing this story, it allows me to express the unexplained occurrences in common people's lives. I have also been a victim of a haunting. Take a journey with me and explore my personal endeavors. I'm a thirty-eight-year-old single good-hearted woman. I want to share this story with all of you, who are willing and is interested in reading about the paranormal. A Myriad of darkness is a modern day romance story filled with paranormal activity. A young woman searches for true love and discover something she could never imagine. It contains adventure, humor, spirituality, horror, and mystery. Her life drastically changes when she finds out her true identity. It is filled with uncanny twists and turns and will keep you at the edge of your seat.

ABOUT THE AUTHOR

Jamila Wiley, was born on February 13, 1974. She is the second eldest of five children. She was born in a small town in Northern California. She is a single woman who graduated from college, as a Medical Assistant. She is a student studying to become a Pharmacist. She enjoys cooking and singing. Her interest are traveling, reading, and hiking. She enjoys spending time with family and friends. She is passionate about nature and wildlife. She hopes one day to fulfill her dreams of becoming a well known author.

BOOK DESCRIPTION

Delve deep into the mystery between good vs. evil. What appears to be ordinary isn't ordinary. Nadia Goldstein is a single thirty-six-year-old woman, who has been unlucky with finding true love. Her biological clock was ticking, and she wants to settle down with Mr. right. Her lonely days were finally over when she met John. They instantly fell in love. She later discovered that he wasn't going to remain faithful to her. She ended her relationship with him, and then she met Boris. When she met Boris, she fell for him. No other man could take his place. Boris was a very gorgeous man who swept her off her feet. He was passionate, caring, and generous. However, he had another agenda. Nadia discovered that Boris has a secret past. Strange and bizarre events soon begin to develop. Her ex-lover comes to her in her dreams and visions seeking something. Supernatural forces are at work. Someone is trying to eradicate her. She is plagued with paranormal occurrences. Doors open and slam shut by themselves, the television turns on and off by itself. Picture frames are hurled across the room and shatters. She begins to question her own sanity and is forced her to confront her past. She has been running for her life and tries to escape. She committed herself into a psychiatric ward to try to escape the terror. Pure evil is lurking and is continuously watching her. A hex has been placed on her life, and she must find a way to undo it before it's too late. She is hunted down by an unknown dark force who wants to derive her soul. She has bizarre dreams that she must quickly learn to decipher. Something eerie and vile resurfaces through an open portal, every anniversary year when it all begins. Hellish nightmares begin to emerge shortly after a separation with her lover. Strange and sinister events begin to develop. Darkness reigns over her. Will she face her ultimate fears? She becomes suspicious of her ex-lover's, who will betray her first?

INDEX

A

astral projection, 28

B

black jacket society, 42
Boris
  breakup with Nadia, 27
  first date with Nadia, 22
  haunting Nadia, 27
  meeting Nadia, 20, 22

C

chakra cleansing, 58

D

Dr. Petersburg, Robin, 47–48

F

Fredrick (man of Nadia's dreams)
  first date with Nadia, 52–53
  meeting Nadia, 50

G

Goldstein, Nadia
  attempting to escape the hospital, 38
  attending group therapy, 47
  background of, 49–50
  being admitted to the psychiatric
    hospital, 34, 46
  being stalked, 41
  breakup with Boris, 27
  confessing to Fredrick about the curse,
    55
  consultation with her psychologist,
    46–47
  consultation with Rick, 28
  eavesdropping Boris's phone
    conversation, 26
  final breakup with John, 19
  first date with Boris, 22
  first date with Fredrick, 52–53
  haunted by Boris, 27
  hiring a private investigator to follow
    Boris, 59
  hospital discharge of, 39
  on intense medication, 37
  meeting Boris, 20
  meeting Fredrick, 50